Tracey Anne Cox has written under a pseudonym to protect identities for the purposes of this book. She was born in 1966 and lived in Bristol all her life. For the past 28 years, she has worked for the local authority. Tracey Anne runs a local Rainbow Guides unit. Tracey Anne has written for fun in the past and produced plays for the Rainbow unit. This is her first book.

I would like to dedicate this book to Dot and Gill for sharing their incredible story and allowing me to put this in word. Also, this is dedicated to the memory of Lil and Barney.

Tracey Anne Cox

# TAKE THEM OR I
# WILL KILL THEM

AUSTIN MACAULEY PUBLISHERS™

LONDON • CAMBRIDGE • NEW YORK • SHARJAH

A CIP catalogue record for this title is available from the British Library.

ISBN 9781528954419 (Paperback)
ISBN 9781528955027 (ePub e-book)

www.austinmacauley.com

First Published (2021)
Austin Macauley Publishers Ltd
25 Canada Square
Canary Wharf
London
E14 5LQ

I would like to acknowledge my dear friend, Marion, who I call my 'adoptive mum'. Thank you for your encouragement with the book and your belief in me.

I want to thank my friend, Tamsyn. Thank you for your support and for allowing me to chatter endlessly about the book. I'd like to acknowledge all my friends whose enthusiasm and encouragement has helped me achieve my dream. Thank you to Austin Macauley Publishers for their work, advice and help in producing this book.

# Prologue

The baby was in her cot, cold, thirsty and unattended. At ten months of age, Diane knew better than to cry, as it never got her anywhere. In fact, where possible, she knew better than to draw unwanted attention to herself. It only resulted in being shouted at, sworn at, or even being given a beating. For her tender age, Diane was very wise, her survival depended on it, and instinct-driven by the wish to live, she ensured her safety.

She didn't know where her mum, Rita, was, as her mum had left the house earlier. Her older brother, Frank, was entrusted to look after her, but he had gone out to play with his brothers and friends. It was the 1950s and there weren't as many rules and restrictions around as to who could look after young children and infants. Sometimes, older sisters or brothers were entrusted with their younger siblings' care.

It was getting dark and she was becoming colder and colder, yet remained still and quiet. She drifted off to sleep.

Later, she was woken by the sound of her dad, Francis. The bedroom door flew open and a shard of light lightened the dingy bedroom. Her dad kicked the bedroom door shut. Diane flinched on hearing the sound of his voice and trembled with fear.

He had someone with him, another woman, not her mum. He pushed the woman on the bed and she giggled. Both were drunk and her dad switched on a bedside lamp. Both, he and the woman, were oblivious to the silent infant, who regarded them from her cot. Feeling curious about this other woman, Diane stood up in her cot, clutching the bars with her small hands. She was wearing just a rag around her for a nappy, which was soggy and smelling, as it had not been changed that day and she wore a grubby vest which was too big and used to belong to her older brother, Frank. Her hair was dishevelled and her body and face were grubby. She had not had a bath; she was rarely bathed. Usually, her bath time routine was a quick wipe to the face and body with a grubby, musty smelling flannel, which acted as the cleaning routine for the whole family. If you looked at her, you could not be blamed for thinking you were looking at a ragamuffin from the 1800s and not Britain in the mid-1950s.

Diane regarded the woman who was lying on her back, her father laid on top of her. The woman had curly brown hair and a heavily painted face. As she caught Diane watching her, she pushed Francis off of her. He groaned in frustration, emitting an unintelligible expletive. The woman sat up and grabbed her handbag. Undoing it, she took out a half packet of ginger biscuits and walked over to the silent infant whose steady gaze was on her. She handed Diane a biscuit, which Diane quickly took before it could be taken away again. Diane was very hungry and began sucking the biscuit. The woman looked at her and said, "Shhhh," then put her finger to her lips.

Diane, intent on her biscuit, ate it quickly whilst the woman joined Francis on the bed. When the biscuit was finished, Diane lay back down. She was no longer interested in her dad and this woman; she knew what they were doing was what she'd seen her mum and dad do many times before. Recently, her mum and dad hadn't been doing 'that' as her mum's stomach was large and she would push her husband off of her when he was becoming amorous.

Later, she was woken by the sound of her dad's voice, urging the woman to leave. "You'd better go now. She'll be back soon."

The woman stayed asleep, so he nudged her awake. She opened her eyes, which looked bleary, "What?"

He was sitting up now and shook her. "Get going, I said. The wife will be back later."

Wide awake now, the woman got out of the bed and hurriedly dressed. As she left, she addressed Francis who was getting out of bed clumsily due to the amount of beer he had drunk the night before. "Bloody charming, that what you are. You don't know how to treat a woman."

Francis looked at her, "Wha…?"

She opened the door and turned her head, "Forget it," and stormed off her heels, making a loud noise on the lino.

After she left, Francis shuffled over towards the cot. Diane lay as stiff as a board, her eyes wide open, keeping them on her father. Decades later, this behaviour would be described by social workers as 'frozen watchfulness'.

Fortunately, this time, Francis just looked at her and walked out of the door. It didn't occur to him to show her any affection or check to see if she needed changing or required feeding. That was a woman's job. As far as Francis was concerned, the only needs he considered important were his own.

As his footsteps grew quieter and quieter, showing that he was further away, Diane let out a sigh of relief and fell asleep.

This was one of Diane's first memories and although she was only very young, Diane recalled that incident in adulthood and the smell of ginger biscuits made her feel nauseous, bringing back that vivid memory.

# Chapter One

Diane was born in the Forest of Dean. Her father, Francis, married a gypsy girl called Rita, and for her former years, they lived in a house which they rented. Frank was the oldest, followed by Diane, Jo, Matthew, John, Jack and James.

Francis had come from a good family, who worked hard, but when he met Rita, he changed. Rita was a rebel and feckless. Due to marrying out of her gypsy heritage, she was disowned by her family.

Francis had a sister called Bet, who lived in Bristol with her husband, Bertie. These were the closest relatives along with Francis and Bet's elderly mother, who lived in the basement of their rented house. Francis's father had died years ago and he agreed his mother could live with them as she had a small pension and this contributed to the rent.

Bet and Bertie were registered blind, even though Bet had sight in one eye. Although they tried to visit as much as they could and bring gifts for the children and had a fairly regular presence in the children's lives, they lived too far away to realise what was happening in the family home.

As a result, the couple was well and truly on their own. Living without the steady advice of their parents, they struggled to budget their money.

Rita didn't seem to realise how to keep a home tidy and clean. She was rebellious and would not have accepted any advice, no matter how kindly it was meant. As a result, any money they had was squandered and gone virtually as soon as Francis had been paid. Ever since Rita first fell pregnant and had her first child, Frank, she never worked again.

Even some of the poorest people in their neighbourhood, with careful budgeting and saving, were able to create a semblance of cosiness in their home. Unfortunately, this was not the case in Francis and Rita's home. Rita didn't know how to make a meal stretch for several days and consequently, the family often went hungry. As their family grew, their limited resources became less and less.

From what Diane could remember, their home was always cold, there was never enough food and their clothes were often dirty and ill-fitting. From an early age, Diane seemed to know not to be demanding and was often quiet so as not to draw her parent's attention to herself. It might have been because she often saw her older brother, Frank, getting a beating, sometimes for the slightest things. Frank was rebellious and seemed to incur the wrath of his father quite often. As he grew older, he learnt to stay out of his parents' way. He would hang around with friends and sometimes bring back food he had stolen. His parents gladly took the food without asking any questions.

Her parents had a volatile relationship and both drank heavily, leaving an unsettling, unpredictable and frightening environment for the children.

It was difficult to judge which was worse, parents being intoxicated or arguing over the fact they had no money to buy alcohol.

Both parents would physically fight one another, especially when intoxicated and didn't realise or care about the impact this would have on their small children. They were oblivious of their young offspring, sometimes to the extent where a child might be caught in the crossfire. There was no remorse from either parent if a child was accidentally hurt and quite often, Rita would shout at the sobbing child, "Well, you shouldn't be in the bloody way. Now shut up!"

When Diane was 11 months old, her younger sister Jo was born, kicking and screaming as if in protest. It was as if this baby knew what her formative years would be like. Unfortunately, their mother seemed to resent Jo immediately. There were no feelings of maternal love coming from her towards the baby. As if sensing this, Jo reacted by often crying and screaming. But Diane loved her. Despite only being a baby herself, a bond formed between the two sisters, which is still strong today. It was unclear why their mother resented little Jo so much. In those days, issues such as postnatal depression weren't really recognised, and it was a case of having to get on with it. Working-class women of that era had too much housework to do, without the labour-saving devices that are around now. Issues like the 'baby blues' were left to the middle to upper-class women, who had more time on their hands. Wealthier women would have had a nanny or a nursemaid to care for their children. For Rita, it was up to her to deal with how she felt. Francis, like a lot of men from that era, felt it was 'women's work' and not a man's place to look after a child, leaving it to Rita. Unfortunately, the situation meant that she harboured resentment towards little Jo.

Although, with the addiction to alcohol and a rather tempestuous relationship their parents had, not much time was given to housework and routines for the children. This meant the home was a grim, cold and drab place. The children's clothes were rarely clean and were ill-fitting. They rarely had baths and only a wipe with a cold, damp cloth was administered. Meals were sporadic and most of the time non-existent due to Francis's wages being spent on beer.

As the years went by, Diane remained her little sister's protector. Unfortunately, the way the family functioned meant that Diane often had to act in this capacity. For some reason, their mother's resentment of Jo remained the same. If it had not been for Diane, Jo could have perished through lack of food or by seemingly being able to ensure her mother's wrath. Their mother was not prone to being 'maternal' as she put her own needs first. Very occasionally, their mother would be a little kinder to Diane, but those times were extremely rare and Diane still suffered her mother's violence if she was angry. Although the children were rarely fed properly, their parents did manage to get food for themselves. Rita rarely cooked, but they would eat pies and have toast and fared far better than their children. Sometimes, Rita would make a bacon sandwich, cutting off the rind. Later, Diane would take the leftover rind for her and Jo to eat. It did little to assuage their hunger but was better than nothing.

Due to both parents spending any money they had on drinking in the pub, the home was extremely sparse. There were no carpets, sheets were used as curtains. The beds had no sheets, only old blankets on them or old coats, and the mattresses were dirty and urine-stained. The winter nights were the worst. Even though the heavy coats covered them in bed, they were still cold. Both girls would huddle together, trying to get warm, but the cold kept them awake until they fell asleep through pure exhaustion and tiredness. Jo was frightened of the dark. After spending so much time in the dark cupboard, the darkness frightened her. She would tremble with fear and even Diane holding her didn't fully assuage the fear the little girl felt.

There were no ornaments or pictures to define the home and the people who lived there. The wallpaper was drab and peeling, and without any carpet, the home was not cosy or homely. There was an old, torn, smelly sofa and matching chair which only their dad could sit in.

One day, Frank sat in the chair whilst his dad was in the kitchen getting a beer. He only did it for a joke to amuse his little sisters. Frank was always daring and seemed brave to Diane who was two years old at the time and was sat on the sofa with Jo, which was propped in the corner.

Frank, with his cheeky grin, was waggling his head, "I'm the boss of the house, haha." When their dad returned, he was furious. He put down the bottle of beer and shouted angrily, pulled Frank by the scruff of the neck and dropped him on the floor. He landed a foot away from Diane. Giving the trembling boy a kick, their dad grabbed his beer, muttering expletives about kids and walked out of the room.

Frank lay on the floor, quietly sobbing, then picked himself up. Looking at Diane and Jo, he rubbed his eyes angrily, muttering, "I bloody hate him," before running out of the house.

Diane shuffled over to the sofa where Jo was sat, crying. Despite being only a year and a half old, she picked up on the

15

anger and sadness, then reacted in the only way she could. So, Diane snuggled up to her and comforted the crying baby, whispering, "shh, shh there, baby." As well as a mothering instinct, the little girl was fearful the cries would wake their mother, who was still in bed, sleeping off the previous night's drinking session. The children knew not to wake her as it would be all the worse for them if they did.

The family home was particularly deprived compared to a lot of families living in the area. What most children took for granted and were used to having had been very different for Diane and her siblings. The children didn't know what a clock was, had never seen a book, held a pencil, or even knew what a bottle of shampoo looked like. They never washed in warm water and generally, the only wash they had was with a grey, stained flannel with soap, if there was any around at the time. Occasionally, they would have a bath, but usually, this was due to relatives visiting and the parents felt they had to make an effort.

Despite the utter privation that the family lived in, when Francis's relatives visited, they felt they had to put on some sort of a show. The children would be bathed in lukewarm water and soap. Rita would sort through the clothing frantically, to find the most respectable looking clothes, which were still too big or small. She would comb their hair. For the girls, this would be particularly hard as their hair was long and tangled. Rita would brush their hair roughly and the girls would cry in pain as their tangled hair was being brushed. If they complained or cried, she would hit them across the head with the hairbrush, muttering, "That will give you summat to cry for." Eventually, as they grew older, Diane learnt not to sob or shout in pain and would bite her lip and keep still, hoping that the ordeal would end soon. But Jo would scream and cry, causing Rita to hit her relentlessly with the hairbrush.

So, although they were cleaner when relatives visited, the ill-fitting clothes still made them look neglected. Rita rarely did any housework and the Ajax powder would come out and Rita would give the worktops a quick wipe, as she didn't want

16

to have the relatives, or in later years, social workers, lecturing her on cleanliness. The floors would be swept and that would be about the extent of the housework. The family didn't have many belongings to clutter the place up. Dirty and clean items of clothing would be stuffed in the airing cupboard.

The house was a three-storey rented home, with their grandmother living in the basement. The children would go to her for comfort after a beating, or to hide from their parents, especially if they had been drinking. Neither parent wanted to bother walking up and down the stairs to the basement. Granny tended to keep herself to herself and didn't get involved with the couple when they argued. Granny was old and frail, and couldn't cope with the arguments, and felt it was better to keep her distance. If the children were lucky, Granny might have a sweet or two for them to eat or a biscuit. Granny had a friend who visited regularly and would bring a cake. She often saved the cake for the children to eat.

At times, the children had to sneak down to see their granny because their mother resented the girls going down to her for solace. Although she didn't have much money herself, apart from a small pension, Granny showed the girls kindness and love, which was something they lacked upstairs with their parents. The only attention the girls had from their parents was negative. All the children learnt at an early age to keep their distance. When their grandmother died, the children missed her sorely.

All the children lacked the basic needs of food and clothes. They rarely had any toys from the parents. Sometimes, they would be given toys or new clothes by their Uncle Bertie and Aunty Elizabeth, who they called Aunt Bet. When Diane was learning to talk, she couldn't say Elizabeth and only said Bet and the name remained the same. Shortly after the visit, their parents would take the toys and clothes to sell in order to buy more alcohol.

After one visit, Jo (aged three years) became the proud owner of a dolly in a pink plastic bath. It was a birthday present from her aunt and uncle. Jo loved and cherished this gift, as it was rare for any of them to have something new. For some reason or other, these toys weren't taken. Possibly because their parents didn't think it would sell for much. So, both girls enjoyed playing with the dolly bath and one doll which was old and managed to survive not being taken and sold. The girls took turns in smelling it, to take in the 'new' smell. Jo would carry the dolly in her bath with her and would take it to bed with her for fear it would disappear. In a life that was drab and dull, the bright pink colour of the dolly's bath was something bright in their grey, sombre lives.

Months later, as winter set in, the children were sat around the fire. For a change, they had the open fire lit. Frank had collected twigs and bits and pieces as they rarely had the money for coal. It was a freezing evening in December and they were jostling each other to get nearer the fire. Their dad was at the pub and mum was in the bedroom lying down, so the children were left to their own devices. As usual, Jo had her dolly in her bath on her lap.

Suddenly, without warning, her older brother Frank grabbed the dolly and bath and threw it on the fire. Jo and Diane gasped in shock. "My dolly! My dolly!" Jo screamed.

Frank turned to her and said, "Well, if you want it, get it."

Jo looked at the fire in fear, her eyes wide and rounded; she moved her arms to grab the dolly and bath, when Diane shouted, "No!" Jo was too young to think of her safety and could only think of her dolly bath, so she plunged her arms in the fire to retrieve her toys. Even Frank, who was known for his 'daredevil' antics, winced and a series of oohs and aahs were emitted from all the children. Little Jo screamed as her arms and legs made contact with the fire and quickly moved them back out of it and touched her legs with her hands. Diane looked in horror at her arms and legs which were red and raw.

The screams and crying brought their mum downstairs. "What the bloody hell is going on here?" The sudden appearance of their mum, who in her anger looked a frightening and menacing apparition, had an instantaneous effect as Frank suddenly fled, leaving just the two girls and their baby brother.

Poor little Jo screamed in agony and was inconsolable and seemed oblivious to her mother. However, Diane was frightened, as she knew their mum never liked being woken up, and somehow in her anger, seemed even more frightening than usual. "Well, come on, tell me, you've woken me up and you better have a bloody good reason."

Rita's eyes bored into the two frightened little girls. Jo was still crying in pain and shock, so it was up to Diane to explain. "Well, Mum, Frank threw Jo's dolly's bath in the fire and Jo burnt her hands trying to get it out."

Their mum glared at them and then sighed, "Well, just put a cloth under the cold tap and put it on her legs. I'm going back to bed." That was it, her mother didn't even check to see how burnt she was, there was no consideration about taking her to a doctor. In fact, her mother barely looked at her.

Although partly relieved as she watched her mother disappear, Diane sensed this was wrong. Only recently, a girl she knew in their street had been out playing and fell down. Upon hearing her cry, the girl's mother had rushed out to her daughter and picked her up, taking her indoors and muttering reassurances as she tried to make the sobbing child feel better. But then, their mother was different, she rarely showed the children any affection. Sometimes she would hug Diane – normally after she had a few drinks, but the hug would be too tight and suffocating and Diane could smell the overpowering smell of alcohol. So, the experience was rarely enjoyable. In fact, Diane had learnt to stay out of her mother's way when she had been drinking. On the other end of the scale, her mother could become really nasty after several drinks and would lash out at whoever was in her path.

Diane thought that just this once her mother would look after Jo properly as she was seriously hurt, but sadly, she showed the usual indifference towards her younger daughter. So, it was up to Diane to take care of Jo's wounds.

There was no sense of trying to help Jo feel better, and no medical advice sought. When their mum went back to bed, Diane led Jo who was sobbing, shaking and seemed to be in shock. Diane dragged a kitchen chair to the sink and helped

Jo climb on to the chair and then the sink. She then ran the cold tap, getting Jo to place her arms under it.

Whilst Diane cupped water to put on Jo's legs, she felt helpless as her sister sobbed uncontrollably. Diane could see her sister's arms and legs going red and blistery and it scared her. As Jo sobbed pitifully, little Diane felt out of her depth. She was scared; she didn't know what to do to help Jo. She wept quietly, wishing that Aunt Bet was there, as she would have known what to do and would have helped them.

The girls shared a single bed and both spent a sleepless night. For Jo was suffering from her burnt arms and loss of her doll's bath, and for Diane having the burden of worrying about her younger sister. She never knew what the irrepressible Jo would do next!

Jo is in her 60s now and still bears the scars of that event.

# Chapter Two

There were seven children altogether growing up in the house. But their mum had a lot of stillbirths and miscarriages. Being the oldest girl, Diane seemed to take on more responsibility, especially for Jo and John.

Frank was the oldest by several years and had since learned to keep out of his parent's way whenever possible.

The back garden was big and their dad often seemed to be digging it up. The boys never really showed an interest but sometimes Diane's interest was piqued and she would go and see what dad was doing. Diane hoped he was gardening and planting flowers, she thought flowers would look nice in the garden and brighten it up. As their lives were drab, for her mum rarely did any housework and didn't appear to know how to wash the clothes probably, hence, the children often wore drab, grey, washed-out looking items of clothing, which often were too small or too large. However, Diane would never dare to complain about fear of arousing her mother's wrath and getting a beating in the process. When Diane saw other girls at school in pretty dresses or smart pinafores, she would sigh and wish, just for once, she would have a pretty dress with matching ribbons like so many of the other girls had and be able to wear smart, polished, shiny shoes.

Diane felt it would be nice to have pretty flowers in the garden, it would brighten up their home by bringing some colour into it, or she could wear flowers in her hair like she once saw in town in the television shop. They didn't have a television at home. They had an old radio which rarely worked and her dad spent hours fiddling about with it to try and get it to work.

Whenever she approached her dad to ask if she could help him with the garden, he would tell her to go away, "Get out of it. Can't you see I'm busy!" Feeling dejected, she would walk away. She didn't question why he would be so impatient with her or why he shooed her away so brutally.

As it happened, Dad never did grow flowers or vegetables, instead, he was burying miscarriages and stillbirths, which were placed in cardboard boxes. At the time, Diane didn't realise this always coincided with her mother staying in bed as she was unwell.

At times, Diane remembered when her mum was pregnant and knew a baby was going to be born, then suddenly the baby bump seemed to disappear, but there was no baby. Diane didn't ask about the baby as her mum would lose her temper. She learnt from an early age not to incur her mother's wrath. Rita had no patience with childish curiosity.

Rita never prioritised caring for her children and this was evident in the home conditions, state of the children and lack of food in the house.

Diane and Jo would wear cardigans too small, and in the winter, would try and stretch the sleeves in a vain attempt to cover their arms. They also either wore ill-fitting shoes or no shoes at all.

Lack of food was a constant in their home and Diane and Jo were often hungry. One time, when their dad was out and mum was asleep, Jo crept into the kitchen and pulled a chair across the floor, making noise in her efforts. Diane looked alarmed and hissed at her, "Shhh, you will wake her up."

Jo looked defiantly at her older sister, "I'm hungry!" she declared loudly.

Diane looked around worriedly as if her mum was going to appear from downstairs. Fortunately, there was no sign of her. Diane said, "I will help you move the chair but don't drag it." Both little girls quietly picked up the chair and moved it across the kitchen. They were a curious sight as Diane was slightly taller with her blonde hair wearing a yellow, stained dress which was too big for her, and Jo with her dark brown hair wearing a blue top which was too small and a green skirt which was big and tied with one of her dad's old ties.

Once the chair was at its destination, Jo climbed on to it, then on to the kitchen cupboard and opened a door. The cupboard was bare, apart from a container and Cow & Gate dried milk.

Jo grabbed the tin and Diane got a spoon. Both girls sat on the cold kitchen floor taking it in turns to share the dried milk, which did little to assuage their hunger. Both girls were hoping that their older brother might be able to bring something home when he came back. Sometimes, he was able to acquire food, either by doing jobs for the shopkeepers or failing that, stealing food.

Both girls often recalled a particular event. When Diane was six and Jo, five, their mum gave Diane an egg. Both girls looked questioningly at her as it was one egg and two children. Jo looked up to ask where was her egg, ignoring the kick Diane gave to her tell her to 'shut up'.

Rita looked at Jo, her face clouded with resentment. Then, ignoring Jo, she turned to Diane and said, "Well, what you leave, she can eat." Their mum walked out of the room. Diane was in a dilemma, she was really hungry, her tummy had been growling for hours now, as she couldn't remember the last time she had eaten. She was hungry enough to eat three eggs, let alone just one. Diane looked at her little sister. Jo was really tiny and looked beseechingly at Diane. Diane sighed to herself. She felt so hungry, but she couldn't eat the egg to herself and let Jo watch. She knew Jo was hungry too, as Jo had complained earlier to their mum, who responded by clipping her ear and shouting at her to go away. Diane's spoon was poised over the egg; she dug the spoon into it and divided the egg between them. She could never resist those doleful looks Jo gave her. So, she shared the egg, even though her own stomach was groaning with hunger. For a child so young, Diane seemed to have a sense of responsibility to her younger sister, which probably ensured Jo's survival.

Diane knew that her mum preferred her to Jo and showed this in some ways. There was a woman who lived several doors away and had three daughters, and often gave Rita the clothes her daughters had grown out of. Rita would sort out the clothes and ensure Diane received the prettier dresses.

From a very young age, Jo had a clear sense of what was fair and unfair and would say what she thought, and loudly at that, which meant Jo often was treated harshly by both parents. Not that any of the children were treated that lovingly, as Diane also got her fair share of being beaten and sworn at. However, Diane had always had that instinct not to say much, to be quiet and watch, Diane was very watchful. But Jo acted on instinct, if she was unhappy or something was not fair, she would let people know, despite the times Diane tried to advise her to be quiet. This might be in the form of telling her to 'shut up', sometimes she needed to give Jo a nudge or a little kick.

Unlike most children who can lose themselves in a fantasy of imagination, neither Diane nor Jo was able to do this. For Diane, she was always looking out for danger and was busy ensuring that both she and Jo were able to survive. With this sense of responsibility, Diane and Jo's childhood was very different. Managing to get through a day with some food in their tummies and being able to find clothes that weren't too dirty and just about fitted was a huge task. At her young age, Diane already had an 'old head on young shoulders'. She cared about being dressed properly. For the boys, it was a different matter, they didn't seem to care what they wore and would run wild. They didn't care if their shorts were torn or grubby. Quite often, shorts and tops would be ripped when they were out playing and fighting, but they didn't worry about it.

# Chapter Three

During the early days, the family lived in a rented house. The owner would come to collect the rent on a weekly basis.

The children's dad worked and was paid on a Thursday. Payday for the parents was the highlight of the week. However, instead of setting aside money for rent and food, they would go to the pub to spend it. Unfortunately, even that didn't seem to make the parents happy, as inevitably, they would come back, worse for wear and end up arguing loudly, which sometimes turned physical. Frank used to think it was funny and would laugh. But he was a little older and just seemed to have the knack of disappearing when things became unpleasant.

However, Jo who always seemed to be in the wrong place at the wrong time and often incurred her parent's wrath, whilst Frank seemingly managed to disappear just in the nick of time.

Quite often when it was time for the rent man to collect the rent, the children would be urged to be quiet and pretend they were not in.

It was a case of woe betide any child who made a noise. Frank normally kept out of the way and would be out with friends playing in the field

One day, their mum warned them when the rent man was due, "Whoever makes a noise will be for it." As if to emphasise the repercussions, she raised a fist. Jo flinched as she had been a recipient of that fist several times.

Their mum addressed Diane, "I'm making you responsible. If any of those buggers makes a sound, you are for it." Diane gulped. Although she could not be sure that her siblings would be quiet, John was just a baby. So, their mum went for a 'lie down' which often preceded a trip to the pub and it was left to Diane to ensure all was quiet. Frank, had conveniently gone out to play.

Half an hour later, there was a loud rap on the door. The children were hidden behind an old settee that had seen better days. She whispered frantically, "Now shush everyone. He will be gone soon and we can play."

Three-year-old Jack looked up, "Play?"

Jo looked cross, "Shut up, Jack." Jack looked crestfallen.

"Don't worry," whispered Diane, "we will play, but at the moment, the game is to see how quiet we can be." Both girls were well aware of the consequences if their younger brothers made too much noise.

Then James said, "Play." Diane hugged him and Jo shushed him, he was only a baby and didn't understand.

The door knocked again and Jo placed her hand over James's mouth which he struggled against and become cross. The children kept so quiet and to their relief, they could hear the retreating footsteps of the rent man.

When they felt it was safe, Diane sighed with relief. "Well, that's him out the way. I'll tell Mum."

There was a sense of relief and feeling that they had succeeded in outwitting the rent man, Diane felt pleased in achieving this mission and when she told Mum the rent man had gone, she just replied, "Well okay, bugger off now. I'm busy." Diane felt a keen sense of disappointment as she had managed to keep the others quiet and this was barely acknowledged.

As she left, she frowned, wondering, "How can you be busy just being in bed?"

Some children might have had a feeling of disappointment, hoping their parent may have praised them for being so clever. However, for Diane and her siblings, this was just the way Mum was, so not worrying about it too much, Diane rounded up her siblings and they played.

Avoiding authorities had become a way of life. It was only when Frank started school that suspicions were raised about his neglected presentation and how thin he looked. Although child safeguarding procedures were different back then, authorities could not fail to notice there were levels of neglect going on. Frank rarely looked clean and his clothes were tatty, well-worn and grey. The family's neighbours would have seen how neglected the children were and knew the parents frequented the pub often, leaving the children to their own devices. However, generally in that area, neighbours would comment to one another about what a 'disgrace' those parents were, but felt that it was the family's business and not their responsibility to intervene. Occasionally, a neighbour might give the girls a jam sandwich or a bit of homemade cake as they felt for the girls. Their sympathies were not so much for the older boy, Frank, who was running wild at the age of four and getting into all kinds of mischief. Apart from family, it was rare for any neighbours or friends to come to the house, and the odd few who did were usually as intoxicated as the parents and would not be in a fit state to recognise the deprivation and poverty in the house.

One afternoon after school, Diane and Jo were in the living room. Their parents were at the pub. Suddenly, their brother appeared. "Quick, hide me from the social worker."

Diane frowned, "What?"

Frank waved his arms in agitation, "Hide me, quick. She's going to put me in foster care." The children had been told tales about foster care, and that it would be a terrible existence with no freedom and frequent beatings, and that they would be separated. Both parents had coached the children about this, ensuring that each child was petrified of the thought of going into care. Although at home they had little to eat and were physically abused frequently, so that would have not been any different. For the children, being separated would have been the hardest part of being in care. Both Jo and Diane were devoted to one another and were terrified at the thought of being apart. The children were young and believed in their parents' tales.

On this occasion, their parents were out at the pub. Diane had to think quickly, "Hide in the chimney."

Frank frowned, "The chimney?"

Diane nodded, "Yes, they won't think to look there."

Jo nodded, "Go on up the chimney," and giggled, thinking it was funny.

Diane shushed her, "Shut up, Jo, it's not funny. You don't want to end up in care, do you?" This was enough to quell her mirth. Diane was Jo's constant companion and she knew they would be lost without each other.

There was a knock at the door. Frank looked worried. Diane nodded at him, "Quick, get up there." Frank retreated to the chimney and climbed up.

Jo answered the door. The social worker was middle-aged with grey curly hair and horn-rimmed glasses. She looked at Jo, "Hello, is your mummy here?" Jo looked nervously at Diane.

Diane responded, "Sorry, our mum is out at the moment."

The social worker stepped into the house uninvited. "That's alright, I will wait. When will she be back?"

Diane looked at Jo then back at the social worker, Diane said, "Err, we don't know. Umm, Granny is sick so she's looking after her."

The social worker regarded the girls. Both looked grubby and ill-kempt. She asked the girls, "Where is Frank?"

Jo looked at Diane and said, "He's out playing, Miss." There was a silence and then the social worker announced she was leaving and told them to tell their mother that she had asked after them and would call in another time.

Once the social worker left, the girls breathed a sigh of relief. Jo called up the chimney, "It's okay, Frank, she's gone."

Frank appeared looking sooty and the girls laughed as you could only see the whites of his eyes. He seemed relieved, "Bloody hell! That was a close one." All the children laughed. They were relieved they had gotten the better of an adult, especially 'a bloody social worker' as their mother would say.

Common sense then reigned and Diane told him to have a wash or Mum and Dad would wonder what happened. All three children giggled nervously, feeling quite empowered that they had outwitted the social worker. They had a succession of social workers visit from time to time and their mother was often derogatory towards them. Their mother would say "She, with her silver spoon in her mouth, what does she bloody know?"

One day, their mother was complaining loudly about the social worker with the 'silver spoon in her mouth' and Jo innocently looked up and said, "But she didn't have a spoon in her mouth, Mum, cos I didn't see it." The others laughed and to their amazement, even their mother laughed with them. Rita rarely laughed with her children, so this was a rare occasion. If Rita had been a caring mother, she would have been able to appreciate her children. Young Frank was a resourceful lad and often managed to get food for his younger siblings, Diane was caring and older for her years, and outspoken little Jo could say the funniest things. Unfortunately, Rita and Francis were too self-absorbed in getting their own needs met and had no inclination or urge to get to know their children properly. Most of the time, the children were seen as an annoyance to Rita and she felt they were often in her way.

Due to the fact that their mother wasn't really home orientated and didn't seem to have the ability to manage and budget, the children were often not fed regularly.

Sometimes, the girls would be made to go to the grocer who was across the road to see if they could get some food on credit. It was always the girls and not the boys. The boys were seen as being cheeky and out of hand, whereas the girls might be able to bring out empathy. Their mum would give them a list and see if they could get some credit. After several incidents where the money was never repaid, the grocer became wise and was not so willing to give them credit. However, when Diane and Jo came in, he could not totally refuse and would somehow find something for them, and sometimes an odd couple of sweets for the girls, or if they were really lucky, a slice of cake.

One day, they were eating a cake in the grocer's and a shopper, Mrs Evans, came in and shook her head, "It's never right, those poor children."

The grocer nodded in agreement. He knew their parents were regular drinkers and that the children went without food. The grocer nodded, "I know, they only think of themselves and having a drink. They'd be better placed feeding and clothing the young 'uns."

Mrs Evans nodded emphatically, "Yes, even when my Len was out of work when he hurt his arm, my children were fed and clothed properly. They didn't do without, even if I had to." Mrs Evans went on to talk about how she made vegetable stew which had to last the family for several days. The grocer suppressed a sigh, if allowed to, Mrs Evans would go on and on, putting the world to rights. Meanwhile, the girls continued eating their cakes. Both girls ate slowly, savouring each crumb as they were sitting on some chairs the grocer had for his more elderly or disabled customers. The shop was warm and welcoming, despite the off draught as shoppers came in and out of the shop. Mrs Evans continued to talk about feckless parents shirking responsibility and how they didn't deserve children.

Eventually, she left after purchasing some items and as the door closed, Jo remarked, "Cor! She can talk!" Diane giggled and the grocer suppressed a laugh and seeing the girls had finished, he suggested they go home as their mother would be worried about them.

He gave them some groceries, which had been in the shop a while, which he didn't think would sell. He had sometimes heard about Francis and Rita's tempers and didn't want to send the girls home empty-handed, as they would suffer the consequences.

Both Diane and Jo enjoyed these treats as they were rarely fed properly by their parents let alone given a treat of sorts. The grocer was kind to the children and seemed to realise the girls weren't fed well, and would often give them something to eat. If they came back with a good amount of food, Rita sometimes seemed pleased. But more often than not, she would complain that there wasn't much food there and grumble she would be better off doing the job herself, although she never did. Both girls were wise enough to eat the cake or sweets as fast as possible before they got home, as the boys would grab the sweets from them.

Sometimes, Diane would be told she was going for a walk with her mum. When Jo asked, "And me too?" their mum would tell her to stay where she was or else. Although she felt a little left out, there was also a degree of relief as Jo never knew when her mum was going to lash out at her.

The first time Rita and Diane went out, they walked to the fields and stopped where there were some boulders. "Sit there on that rock," her mum commanded. Diane saw down immediately; she knew not to argue or ask why. Then, to her surprise, her mum handed her a small bag of sweets and said, "You stay here, alright? You got your sweets. I won't be gone long." As her mother walked away Diane could see a man walking towards her, they started talking to each other and then walked side by side into the woods. Diane would sit patiently waiting and savouring the sweets which were a real treat. Diane never asked why her mum went into the woods with the man, who had never spoken to her. She just enjoyed the rare treat. When her mum returned, she would look at Diane and command, "And not a word to your father, alright, or you will get this." She would raise her arm as if to hit Diane. Diane shrunk back and was cowering with fear. Rita laughed, loud and raucously. To a young child, this was strange behaviour; one minute Mum was giving her a rare treat and the next threatening to wallop her. It was very confusing for the little girl. Rita was so unpredictable it was difficult to tell how she would react. Diane followed her mother home in silence, thinking, *grown-ups are strange.* She would then cheer up and look forward to Jo's joyful face when she presented her with some of the sweets, she saved for her.

Quite often, the children's parents would be in the local pub, The Swan Inn. If the family had been out, they would stop at The Swan so the parents could go and have a drink, leaving the children outside. If the weather was good, they would play and it didn't seem so bad, but if it was cold, rainy or snowing the children would shiver and huddle up together to keep warm. None of them had adequate coats or clothing to fend off the cold, and the time seemed to take ages before their parents came out of the pub. The parents never thought to buy them a drink or crisps. They just had to wait outside whatever the weather was doing.

Passers-by would shake their heads and tut muttering words like, "It's a real shame for those kiddies." It was unclear why their parents sometimes insisted on bringing them to the pub, only to leave them outside.

Winter was always a problem and there never seemed to be enough coal to put on the fire. The children would be sent to collect coal and if there was no coal, they would be cold. Even in bed, it was freezing cold with only old musty smelling blankets. Diane and Jo would huddle together in order to try and keep warm. The house was old with no heating, apart from the living room fire, which was rarely lit. Sometimes, ice would appear on the inside of the windows.

Often in winter, the boys would go out to the woods to salvage twigs and branches for the fire. Frank was good at lighting the fire. Often, their parents were in the warmth of the pub, leaving the children cold and hungry.

# Chapter Four

The children's mother was from gypsy origin and the children didn't have contact with her family, with the exception of a maternal uncle who occasionally visited when they lived in the house. Rita's parents had died before Diane was born, so they never knew them.

However, they did have contact with their dad's sister and her husband – Bet and Bertie. They would visit and bring gifts and food and clothes. The girls really loved the visits where they were paid attention and sometimes given gifts and always got something good to eat. Uncle Bertie was blind and had a lot of patience with the children and would sit with them, telling them stories. Aunt Bet would talk to the children and show an interest in what they were doing, which was a stark contrast to how their parents were. Bet and Bertie were the few adults in their lives who showed them affection. Jo and Diane would feel safe and protected in their arms.

Uncle Bertie had become blind from measles when he was 21. When he told them stories, it brought them a new, exciting world of fun, which was a contrast to the stark reality which faced them every day.

With them came food and treats, such as chocolate, biscuits and sweets. For children who were rarely fed any meals, the treats were something they enjoyed and for a short while, at least the poverty, neglect and brutality of their daily lives ceased. Once the treats were gone and the children were hungry, they would talk about how wonderful those treats tasted and wished their aunt and uncle would visit more often.

As well as the treats and gifts, the children enjoyed having adult attention which was positive; being asked questions about their favourite colour or about school or what games they liked to play and also being cuddled. It was such a contrast to the attention their parents gave them. They never really talked to them and only communicated by shouting, swearing and beating them. When Jo was a year old, she would freeze with fear if an adult tried to cuddle her as she had only known physical abuse.

Her freezing in fear, however, worried Bet and made her wonder why Jo was like this. She once broached the subject with Rita, who was defensive and just said that was the way she was. Bet would describe this to Bertie when they got home from a visit. Bet would fret that, "Something wasn't right," but couldn't work out what it was.

Their parents would put on a show and explain any injuries seen as accidents or rough play between the children. As Jo grew older, she realised that her aunt and uncle wouldn't harm her and eventually stopped freezing with fear and learnt to enjoy the cuddles and affection.

Seeing her aunt and uncle cuddle her siblings reassured the little girl that she would not come to any harm.

Although both felt something was amiss, they had no idea of the extent of deprivation and abuse going on in the home. For Rita always put on a show and would grab Diane and Jo in a rough type of hug as if she was being motherly, which sometimes confused the girls, as they were more used to her lashing out at them. Rita never invited Bet and Bertie upstairs to see the bedrooms with the urine-stained mattresses which were covered in old overcoats. The living room was sparse and was so lacking in ornaments and toys that she didn't really have to work hard to keep it tidy.

Gradually, Jo learnt that not all adults were like her parents, that some adults were kind and gentle. Eventually, by watching Diane and her brothers being cuddled, Jo learnt to trust a little more. However, she never lost her fear of her parents and would still freeze with fright if they approached her.

Bertie enjoyed telling the children stories. As he got older, Frank would choose to go off playing with his friends, but Diane, Jo and the younger children hung on to the stories.

Uncle Bertie had a way of putting their names in the stories which made them feel special. To the girls, to listen to Bertie's stories and sucking a sweet was bliss. There was a particular story Bertie told about the girls walking in the woods and encountering a wicked witch, but with all his stories, the girls would be rescued and all would turn out well. Diane sometimes wondered if she would be rescued eventually and would daydream about this.

Both Bertie and Bet showed an interest in the children and the girls especially enjoyed the attention. As they grew older, the girls knew not to get too excited about toys and clothes that Bertie and Bet brought them for their birthdays and Christmas. They knew as soon as their kindly aunt and uncle left, the items would be taken by their mother and later sold.

One day, when Jo had her 4$^{th}$ birthday, she was brought a pretty red and white dress. Bet helped her try it on and she loved the feel of the soft, clean material against her skin and the smell of the newness as it was rare for her to wear anything new. Bet smiled at her niece; with her dark brown hair, the red suited her.

"Oh, you look so pretty," Diane exclaimed. Jo smiled, enjoying the attention.

Bet nodded and added, "Yes, that's lovely, the colour suits you. What do you think, Rita?"

Rita had been looking away, totally disinterested in her daughter. Rita looked at her and didn't comment, then walked up to her and said, "Well, better get this off of you now, and you don't want to make it dirty, do you? We will keep it for best."

Jo scowled in annoyance, "No, I like it, I want to wear it."

Rita curbed the urge to slap her daughter in front of their relatives. She grabbed Jo roughly and took the dress off Jo, who was sobbing. When Rita walked out of the room with the dress, Jo ran to Bet who lifted her on her lap and tried to comfort the distressed girl. Diane sat quietly; she knew Jo would pay dearly for the outburst once their aunt and uncle had gone. Bet tried to comfort the distressed girl, saying that Mummy was keeping the dress for best and she would wear it. The girls never saw the dress again. Later, when the relatives left, Jo was given a beating and dragged by her hair and thrown in the dark cupboard as a punishment.

The parents didn't show any interest in what the children were doing. They were happy as long as they weren't in their way and gave the children free rein. Frank often ran wild, going out until all times. The parents didn't really worry as long as he was out of the way. However, Diane had a sense of what was right and wrong, so Diane and Jo's existence differed. Mealtimes were ad hoc and only happened if there was food in the house and there were no set bedtimes. Diane and Jo still tended to go to bed early and would play in their bedroom as they wanted to be away from their parents.

One day, the children were in one of the bedrooms. They had been banned there by their dad because Frank was being 'cheeky.' As a result, all children were made to go upstairs with no tea and a hard smack.

The children were completely bored as they had no games and hardly any toys to play with. Jo was in the windowsill, looking out of the window, when Matthew said, "I dare you to jump."

Diane glared at him, "Shut up, don't be silly." Jo looked at them.

Matthew urged her on, "Well, she wouldn't anyway, she's chicken!"

Jo glared at her brother, "No, I'm not!"

Jo went to climb out of the window. Diane pulled her back urging "Don't, it's just a silly dare, don't be daft."

Matthew jutted his chin out, "She won't, she's chicken."

Jo glared at him, "I'm not," and suddenly jumped out of the first-floor window. All the children gasped in surprise and Jo screamed in pain upon landing.

Diane glared at Matthew, "Why did you do that, stupid?"

Matthew shrugged, "Didn't think she'd do it."

Diane pushed him roughly, "You know what she's like. What if you have killed her?"

Frank added, "Yeh, if you killed her, you would end up in prison."

Matthew looked worried and his lip trembled.

Diane and Frank rushed downstairs to see if Jo was alright. Jo was crumpled in a heap, crying in pain "Jo, Jo are you alright?"

Jo looked at her, "I'm not dead but it bloody well hurts!"

Diane raised a tentative smile, relieved her little sister wasn't dead and chided, "Don't swear."

Jo looked confused, "But Mum and Dad do."

Diane put an arm around her, "Yes, but it doesn't mean we have to." Jo nodded though, not quite understanding. Fortunately, Jo was only badly bruised. Jo was really impulsive and often managed to get into trouble. Diane helped her sister upstairs and gently scolded her, "Just cos the boys dare you, it doesn't mean you need to do it." Jo didn't reply, she was sobbing with the pain and couldn't summon up the energy or will to answer her sister back.

Diane made the others promise not to tell their mum that Jo had jumped out of the window. Diane felt her mother would not have cared and might have punished Jo as well with a beating.

Social services became involved again and it was concerns around the family and in particular, Jack, who had learning difficulties and was seen as more vulnerable. Due to the concerns, Jack was placed in a children's home. Jack was born with special needs and deemed more vulnerable than the other children. He, later, was fostered and the carers were to adopt him. Everything seemed set for a better future for him. Then one day, the social worker visited to pass on the sad news that Jack's prospective adopters died. However, Jack never returned to the family home and remained in foster care.

Diane noticed that when the social worker, Mrs Long, was due to visit, their mum was a little keener to get them clean and in their tidiest clothes. The children would be warned of the consequences if they disclosed anything about home life and were told not to trust the social worker.

Diane was torn as the social worker was always kind and spoke nicely. Sometimes, she even gave them a sweet or a lollipop which was a rare treat for the children. The girls had been present on several of her visits. Their mum would seem different and didn't shout in front of the social worker. On one occasion, Jo remarked, "Our mum is talking nice to us." This was said in genuine surprise and not out of sarcasm, as she would have been too young to think of that. Their older brother Frank giggled. Later, when the social worker left, their mum's 'motherly tones' went back to the usual shouting and she clipped Frank across the ear and slapped Jo's legs.

Jo wailed in surprise and pain. Diane and Jo could not understand why their mum had done this. Diane frowned, "Why did she do that?" whilst Jo continued to sob.

Frank explained as he ruefully rubbed his head, "Well, that social worker could get us taken away to see. So, when she's here, our mum pretends she's being nice." Diane frowned and didn't quite understand. Frank continued, "That's why Jack went away to those people who want to adopt him, cos he was special."

Diane asked, "But is he coming back here to live after?"

Frank stood up, shrugged, "I dunno" and ran off out to play.

The children were constantly warned by their parents not to say anything to the social worker and were made to feel they had to be wary of being taken away like Jack was taken. The girls both had mixed feelings about the social worker following their brother Jack going into care.

As it was a threat from their mother that they would go into care and be beaten daily and locked up in a cupboard, with Jack being placed in care, it seemed their mother was right.

Ironically, the gory tales their mother told them were similar to the life they currently had with their parents. However, both Diane and Jo dreaded being separated. Despite their differences, both girls loved each other and it was their love that kept the little girls going and was one of the few positive parts of their fear-filled existence. Their relationship with the boys was different. The boys seemed to go off and do as they liked and appeared to have more freedom.

However, in time, Mrs Long gained their trust and would take them on picnics with her own children. The first time they went on a picnic, Diane tried to find the best clothes that they had. As they were dressing, Jo asked, "What's a picnic?"

Diane frowned, "You will soon see," covering up the fact she didn't know either.

Mrs Long, with her son and daughter who were both older than the girls, arrived and they walked to the local fields and found a spot. Mrs Long's children; Archie and Annie, pulled out the blanket. Jo looked up, "What's that for?"

Annie grinned, "It's to sit on."

Both girls sat down and Jo lay on the blanket and sniffed it, "Cor! That smells better than our blanket at home, don't it, Diane?" Mrs Long's children giggled, but she kept discreetly quiet and seemingly didn't hear Jo's comment. Diane shushed her little sister crossly. Even at her tender age, Diane seemed to know her sister shouldn't be saying such things. Jo glared at her sister defiantly. Mrs Long then uncovered the basket she had been carrying and took out dainty triangular sandwiches, boiled eggs, a large pork pie, big red tomatoes, apples, Chelsea buns and squash for the children and a flask of tea for Mrs Long. Both girls looked at the feast in awe.

"Tuck in then, girls," Mrs Long prompted. Jo looked at Diane who tentatively picked up a sandwich and did likewise. The first bite of the cheese sandwiches felt like heaven to the two girls who had not eaten since the night before. Both took big bites out of the dainty sandwiches.

Archie laughed, "Gosh! We better get a move on, Annie, or there will be none for us."

Mrs Long gave her son a look and told him, "Leave them alone." She then addressed the girls, "Carry on eating, girls, there's plenty of food." Both girls picked up another sandwich, they could not believe how big this feast seemed. They had not been offered so much food in such a long time. Diane watched how Mrs Long and her children ate daintily and tried to mimic this, though the hunger pangs in her stomach were urging to her grab and eat as quickly as she could.

After eating, although they all felt really full, Jo laid down on the blanket and sighed blissfully, "I'm bloody full now." Diane kicked her and shushed her, glaring ferociously at her, but Jo didn't care, she was happy after such a feast, and Diane telling her off wasn't going to dim that pleasure.

Annie took out a ball and they played catch and various games.

The girls didn't know how to play the games but Annie and Archie patiently explained how to play.

As well as enjoying the lovely food, the children thrived by having positive adult attention. Both girls enjoyed being asked questions and for their opinions, no one at home had ever shown an interest. None of the family knew what Jo's favourite colour was or that Diane loved roses.

When Annie asked Diane what her favourite colour was, she frowned and looked puzzled. "Colour?" she asked confused.

Mrs Long quickly realised the little girl's dilemma. "Now, let me see. I think you would like yellow, like that dandelion." Diane blinked, still confused. None of the children knew what colours were. Having parents that never really spoke to them or pointed out colours or counted numbers, both little girls were oblivious to what a colour was. Their parents weren't interested in any of the children. Once Frank was old enough, they would send him to go out on errands, but never had any real conversation with the children. The main dialogue between the parents and the children was normally to order them to do something or telling them to get out of the way.

Normally, if an adult paid them attention, it was shouting followed by a beating or being pulled by the hair to be locked in the cupboard or clipped around the ear. Jo and Diane went to several other picnics and outings with Mrs Long, who seemed to care about them and showed an interest in them. Without knowing it, the girls both learnt good manners and how things should be done, which was different from how things were at home. They started to learn about colours and nature and the names of flowers. Mrs Long did try giving the girls some clothes Annie had grown out of, but Rita resented this because she was a social worker and felt she was interfering. She did sometimes bring them hair ribbons and would spend time brushing their hair and putting ribbons in it. At first, the girls were frightened, recalling how brutal their mother could be with the brush when she occasionally brushed their hair prior to a visit from Bet and Bertie. However, Mrs Long patiently and slowly brushed the knots out and tried to reassure them she would not hurt them.

Despite these outings and kindness shown by Mrs Long, the sense of mistrust of the social workers was still there.

# Chapter Five

Diane started school at age five, and a year later, Jo joined her. They didn't need to wear a uniform but it was still difficult to find clothes that were clean and fitted them.

Although school days were supposed to be 'the happiest days of your life', that was not the reality that Jo and Diane experienced. They were often teased about their clothes, as they were often wearing clothes which were too small, too big or were grubby and threadbare. They rarely had anything that matched and it was difficult for the girls to find clothes that fitted and were clean. They were rarely bought new clothes and lived on hand-me-downs or second-hand gifts from family.

One day, the girls were on their way to school and Jo bent over to re-do her shoe. Suddenly, loud taunts were heard from another child, "Ooh, she's not any knickers on."

This was soon joined in by other children, "Yuk, they got no knickers on."

Diane blushed and grabbed Jo's hand, urging her to stand up quickly. Jo turned to the mocking children, "Oh bloody well, shut up, you lot."

Diane chided her, "Don't swear, Jo."

Jo frowned, "But Mum and Dad swear."

Diane wagged her finger at Jo, "Well, just cos they do, doesn't mean we can swear." Due to being taught good manners at school, Diane had soon realised that not all children had parents who swore, and realised it was something to be discouraged.

Not one of the other children understood the complications and the fact that the girls struggled to find something to wear every day. In those days, unless you went to a private school, children didn't wear a uniform. For the girls, it was a daily struggle to find anything that was relatively clean to wear and often the clothes were too dirty to wear. As a result, the girls would often miss school.

Quite often, the girls would be wearing clothes that were for children a couple of years younger. Some of the girls in the class wore pretty dresses and had ribbons matching the colour of the dress. Both Jo and Diane would have loved to wear such pretty clothes and have ribbons to match, but it was unlikely they would ever be bought ribbons let alone a dress. One day, a girl called Alice was wearing a sky blue and white dress with puff sleeves and the skirt billowed out, she had her hair in pigtails with matching blue ribbons. As they walked home from school, Diane said to Jo, "I wish I had a dress like that. It's so pretty."

Jo nodded, "Me too. Wish Mum would buy us dresses like that instead of this rubbish." Jo pulled at her torn blue dress in disgust.

Diane looked dreamy, "Maybe one day, Jo."

Jo screwed up her face in disgust, "Fat chance."

Diane encouraged Jo to hurry up to get home, "You never know, Mum might have got some stale bread from the baker."

Diane enjoyed school as long as she could keep spiteful taunts from the other children at bay. Her solace was in the classroom, which was a calm place to develop and learn, unlike the teasing and taunts in the playground. Her teacher was kind and often spoke to her after school. However, Diane had an inner sense of not divulging too much information Sometimes, after a particularly bad beating, their mum would tell them if they told, they would get it worse. If the girls sustained an injury to the face or arm where it might be seen, she would tell them to say it was Frank who did it and not their parents. This ensured Diane's silence; however, Jo was more honest and would say the odd thing that would raise concern.

Jo was impulsive by nature, and one day had come into school with a large bruise on her shin. Her teacher, Mrs Bessell, noticed and looked concerned and asked, "Oh dear me, Jo. That's a big bruise you have there. You have been in the wars."

Jo looked at the teacher's kind face. Normally she was used to adults shouting or frowning, but Mrs Bessell was one of the kindest and gentlest teachers in the school and more motherly than her own mother. Jo then said, "Yeh, our mum kicked me and it bloody hurts!" Diane looked horrified, knowing this disclosure could lead to trouble if their parents knew one of them had said anything; it would be likely they'd be beaten black and blue.

Diane addressed Mrs Bessell, "Err, she means our brother, not mum. See, we were playing a game of mummies and daddies and Jo called Frank Mum. It was a joke, see? Frank got really mad cos Jo kept saying mummy, mummy. So, he kicked her, you see." Mrs Bessell nodded slowly and let the girls go. There was a nagging doubt. The girls and their brother often had injuries. With the boys, some of these were due to the rough and tumble that they were involved in with other boys. But the girls' play tended to be more gentle such as hopscotch or skipping. She watched the girls walking away with Diane holding on to Jo's hand. She felt a lump to her throat, thinking how sad it was that they didn't have pretty dresses like some of the other girls. Both Jo and Diane tended to wear faded, washed-out dresses which were either too big or too small. Mrs Bessell had heard rumours about the parents drinking and knew that their father's work was hit and miss. Unfortunately, Francis was often out of employment due to his lifestyle of drinking and could be an unreliable worker.

Meanwhile, once out of the teacher's sight, the girls stopped and Diane rounded on Jo. "What did you say that for, silly?"

Jo jutted out her chin rebelliously retorting, "Well, it's true."

Diane nodded, "Yes, I know that but what happens if our mum and dad find out you told Mum kicked you. We would have Social Services on our back again." (Diane often heard her parents arguing about this and her dad would remonstrate with her mum if she'd marked any of the children, especially the girls as the boys were wild and their bruises could be explained away).

She recalled them having a big row months ago when Jo had a huge bruise on her cheek. In a fury, their mum had punched Jo in the face. When their dad got home, he had started shouting at Rita, "We will have them, bloody social workers, on our backs again, prying into our business, talking to the kids and telling us what to do. It took ages last time before we were shot of the buggers!" Their dad then examined Jo's face and turned to his wife, "Well, there's no covering that up. Nothing for it, you will have to keep her home from school for a few days."

Rita frowned, "Bloody hell." She glared at the two terrified girls who were wide-eyed with fright. Rita addressed the girls, "Get out of my sight now." The girls fled out of the way to their bedroom.

When Diane recalled this, Jo's feistiness had disappeared and she looked white with fear. Diane hugged her, "Don't worry I don't think Miss will do anything," whilst biting her bottom lip and hoping she was right.

One afternoon, the girls came home from school and were playing in their room. As they didn't have many toys, they relied on their imagination. Diane had a good imagination and would daydream about a life of luxury with nice things to wear and eat, whereas Jo's imagination was more for adventure and no school! Suddenly, they heard a knock on the door and their mum answered it and it was one of the teachers. The girls looked at each in shock, it was unheard of to have a teacher visit the home. Jo looked up, "It's Mrs Bessell."

Diane grabbed her arm. "Shh. Follow me."

The girls crept to the top of the stairs to listen. The teacher was talking to their mum about them. She was expressing concern about their shabby clothes and they never had a packed lunch. Jo looked hopeful, thinking this might mean they would be fed, but Diane stopped her, she knew better. Rita kept a rather strained smile on her face, "Well, I do give them a packed lunch, so I don't know what they do with it. Diane is so fussy, if she doesn't like anything, she will throw it away." Rita continued, "As for their clothes, they always have clean clothes at the start but I don't know what they do to get the clothes so dirty."

Jo gasped in surprise and was about to open her mouth and tell the truth when Diane suddenly put her hand over her mouth. She started to lead Jo out of the room, "We're going out to play, Mum." Rita glared at Jo with her eyes narrowed and spoke volumes of the punishment Jo would get if she didn't keep quiet.

Later, the teacher left and the girls were called back inside by their mother who demanded, "What have you been saying? Your teacher seems to think I don't feed you. Well???" She loomed over the girls in a threatening manner.

Jo jutted out her chin, "Well, we don't get fed that much." She received a slap across the face, and enraged, Rita grabbed her by the hair and dragged the screaming girl to the cupboard. Diane watched in horror, despite seeing this punishment often meted out to Jo for her cheekiness, it never failed to horrify her. Seeing her sister hurt really upset the little girl who felt helpless and unable to protect her. No matter how many times she advised Jo to keep quiet, Jo's impulsive nature wouldn't allow her to hold her tongue. Both girls had long hair and this punishment was given to both.

The boys were lucky in that respect as they had really short hair. If the boys were put in the cupboard, they would be dragged by their ears. As a part of survival, Frank would sometimes joke his ears were ten times bigger than they should be with the amount of pulling they received.

But Frank was getting bigger and more daring and seemed to know when to escape to the streets when his parents were angry or drunk.

# Chapter Six

Sometimes, the children and their father would visit his sister, Aunt Winnie, who lived in a crown cottage deep in the Forest of Dean. The girls loved visiting their aunt and seeing the cottage. Compared to their stark living conditions, the cottage was pretty with whitewashed walls and a thatched roof. All the front windows had window boxes with pretty geraniums. Both girls appreciated the prettiness of the cottage. Inside the cottage was small, but cosy. The chairs and settee had pretty lace draped over the top and on the arms. Around the cottage were photographs of the family in assorted frames and a vase of fresh flowers giving the place a cosy and comforting feel, which was a stark comparison to the grime and cold living conditions of their own home, which didn't have flowers, pictures or ornaments to make the place look homely.

Aunt Winnie would greet the children lovingly, hugging them and asking them questions, showing an interest in them. Their father would sit quietly watching them, almost as if he was daring them to disclose the abuse and poor living conditions they endured. Diane was wise to this, and never said anything that would cause their aunt concern; however, sometimes Jo would blurt out something. When she did this, their father would glare in their direction. Diane was a quick thinker and would make out that Jo was just making things up and explained away saying it was a game of make-believe. She knew if she didn't stop Jo, it would be all the worse for both of them and mean a beating from their father and later their mother when he told her what had been said.

Winnie would give them a glass of milk and a slice of homemade cake, which, to them, was wonderful. Diane would resist the urge to gulp the cake down in one go to assuage the ever-present gnawing hunger in her stomach. She liked to make it last, whereas Jo would eat hers quickly and then look hopefully at her older sister for some of her cake.

Aunt Winnie would get the children to play in the garden or let them go into the kitchen and lick the tin of condensed milk. Both girls loved this and it felt like it was Christmas, going to Aunt Winnie's house.

Winnie had chickens and would let the girls collect the eggs. She would put some of the eggs for them in a box to take home. For the girls, this was a real treat and a feast compared to their normal diet.

Their aunt would talk to their father who would eventually get her to lend him some money, although he never paid it back. Aunt Winnie would lecture him and inevitably ask, "When are you going to get your act together? You have four children now, and another on the way?"

Francis would nod and agree in order to get the money from his sister, "I know, Win, but the jobs just aren't around."

Winnie would wag her finger at him and admonish him, "You should never have got together with Rita, she's not good for you and those poor children." Diane walked into the living room and heard Aunt Winnie continuing, "and the state of those children. Those clothes are a disgrace. Can't Rita make them clothes or knit some cardigans, at least?"

Diane looked down at her grubby green check dress with tears in her eyes. Her aunt's comments forced her to really look at herself and Jo properly. "No wonder the kids tease us at school. We look like ragamuffins." She felt a little stung by her aunt's remarks as she had tried to get both herself and Jo as clean and tidy as possible. But without hot water and soap, it was hard to get the grime off of them. She had been pleased to find some elastic bands for their hair and had pulled Jo's hair into two lopsided pigtails and her own blonde hair into a ponytail which had now gone askew.

Aunt Winnie continued to berate her brother who gave excuse after excuse. In the end, she said, "I won't waste time arguing with you, you always end up with the last word anyway! You seem to have an excuse for everything. It's not just yourself you need to think of, it's those poor children."

Going to Aunt Winnie's was one of the few pleasant memories the children had. Despite Winnie's bluntness and berating their father, Winnie had a kind heart, and although she couldn't do much about the situation, she would ensure when the children visited her, they came home with a full tummy. Unfortunately, Winnie thought the only problem was lack of money which resulted in the children's neglected appearance; she had no idea of the physical and verbal abuse the children endured.

The only other pleasure the girls had were visits from Aunt Bet and Uncle Bertie. These three adults showed the children love and kindness which was such a difference to the neglect, abuse and indifference they suffered at the hands of their parents. Unfortunately, the children didn't see their relatives that often, so the care, love and generosity from these relatives were few and far between.

The girls would cling to these good memories when things were intolerable at home. After a visit, at bedtime, both girls would recall their visit. Diane talked about the fruit cake they had eaten, "That cake was so yummy, I wanted it to last forever."

Jo sighed, "Me too. It was bloody lovely."

Diane nudged her sister, "Don't say bloody, it's a swear word."

Jo sat up in bed and folded her arms, "Well, you just said it," and jerked her chin up in defiance. Diane responded by saying she was just pointing out what the swear words were, which didn't count. Jo laid back down, "You always have to have the last word," which was often what Aunt Winnie would say to their father.

Diane turned on her side and muttered sleepily, "Just go to sleep now, Jo." There was no response, Jo was already asleep.

Jo had a fear of the cupboard where she was often dragged by the hair to be locked in the dark. It didn't help when Frank would say that there are giant rats in there that would eat her.

The poor little girl would be terrified. Often, after locking her in the cupboard, their mother would go out or upstairs. Diane would sit on the other side of the cupboard door and try to calm her distraught sister down. She would remember the stories Uncle Bertie told them and recount them to Jo, or sing the nursery rhymes that Aunt Bet taught her. Eventually, Jo would calm down, reassured that her sister was not too far away. Jo tended to receive this form of punishment more often than her sister. Mainly due to the fact that she would answer her mother back. Jo had a keen sense of what was fair and what was not, and really could not help herself. So, if she felt something was not right, she would say it outright. Whereas Diane would hold her tongue, although she felt things were not right and fair, she wouldn't say as much. Apart from the odd times when she felt their mother was being unfair to Jo.

On one occasion, their mother was upstairs, sleeping off the alcohol she had drunk earlier on at lunchtime. It was a Saturday and their brother Frank was in one of his annoying moods and kept teasing Jo, verbally at first and then he kept poking her. When Jo shouted, "Leave me alone!" and screamed, they heard their mother shout from upstairs and her heavy footsteps on the stairs.

Frank fled to get out of the way and their mother grabbed Jo by the hair and screamed at her, "Bloody shut up!"

Diane looked in horror as their mother held Jo by the hair as Jo was dangling with her feet off the ground. So, Diane pleaded with her mother, "Please, Mum, put her down, you are hurting her. It was Frank who made her shout, it's his fault!"

Their mother dropped Jo, who was in a heap and sobbing, and swiftly grabbed Diane by the hair, "Bloody kids, I never get a chance to rest without someone spoiling it." With that, she pulled Diane by the hair and locked her in the cupboard. As she passed Jo, she grabbed her by the dress and threatened her with a beating if she heard another peek out of her. Then she strode out of the room and upstairs. When she felt the coast was clear, Jo crept over to the cupboard and whispered, "Diane, are you alright? I'm sorry."

Diane whispered back from the cold, dark and scary cupboard, "It's okay. I'm alright. Just play quietly and don't wake her again."

Jo sniffed, "I can't play by myself. There's nothing to do."

Diane replied, "Just make up a game and play." Jo said she couldn't so Diane told her a story and eventually little Jo was curled up and fell fast asleep outside the cupboard.

Sometimes, when they were in bed and too cold and hungry to sleep, they would talk about their favourite times and recall good things such as when the grocer gave them a cake or a visit from Uncle Bertie and Aunt Bet. The pleasant memories gave them a little respite from their stark reality and then they would sleep. Diane was good at making up stories and make-believe games. None of the children owned a book, but when Diane learnt to read books herself, she would recall the stories she loved and would repeat them to Jo and make up stories from the tales she remembered. A game both girls enjoyed was imagining they lived somewhere else, where there was money, where parents were kind to their children, where they were fed properly and had new clothes which fitted. Most of the time, the girls wore second-hand clothes which were too big. Both girls were so small for their ages due to lack of nutritious food and would wear clothes that were for children well below their age.

Diane liked to imagine they had been given to their parents by mistake, and that one day their real parents would rescue them from the brutality of their existence and they would have nice food to eat, be showered with kindness and not cruelty and would be able to wear clean clothes that fitted.

The terrors and deprivation of their lives would overtake them and sometimes Jo would have nightmares about being locked in the cupboard and being eaten by giant rats or when she went into the fire to rescue her dolly's bath. Sometimes, Jo would wake screaming and sobbing and their parent would bang on the wall, shouting at them, "Shut up, or I'll give you something to cry for."

Diane would wake up and comfort her sister, saying, "Hush now, you just had a nightmare."

All the time, Diane was thinking and wondering when their permanent nightmare of a life would end. Silent tears would fall down her cheeks at the helplessness of the situation.

Diane, at age five, was to notice how other families treated their children. She witnessed toddlers and babies being cradled lovingly by their mothers and fathers. She often saw other children walking down the street with their mother or father holding their hand, or walking with an arm around the child. Although their parents rarely showed them any kindness or warmth, the children did know what it was like as Aunt Bet, Uncle Bertie and Aunt Winnie could cuddle them, or hold their hands and pick them up. But those interactions were few and far between as they didn't see their relatives that often. Sometimes, when Jo was asleep, Diane would cry herself quietly to sleep as she ached for someone to love her and care for her and her sister. For as much as Diane loved her younger sister, she was only a small girl herself and wanted someone to take care of her and love her as well.

Fiery in nature and seemingly unafraid of the consequences, Jo often had nightmares due to her experiences and forever getting into trouble.

However, some nights, Jo's nightmare would be when she wasn't asleep but awake. From age four, she recalled her dad coming into the room, Diane was fast asleep next to her. He stood over her and placed his finger to his lip to tell her to be quiet, then pulling back the old blanket, he lifted her nightie and started touching her. Jo didn't understand what he was doing but somehow, she knew it was wrong and felt uncomfortable. This soon became a regular thing and Jo started dreading bedtime. Before that, going to bed seemed safer, out of the way of her parents, but now there was this new nightmare. Jo would try and pretend to be asleep in the hope that this would put him off but it didn't. Jo wondered, "Why did he do this to her and not Diane? Was it because Diane was a good girl and not cheeky?"

After several nights of this happening, Jo resolved to try and be better and not cheek her parents. It was difficult to bite her tongue and accept the unfairness of their existence as silently as Diane did. After a day of really being quiet, where even Diane kept looking at her and wondering why she was so quiet. That night, the girls went to bed and Jo settled down to sleep, thinking she had been a good girl and nothing nasty would happen. Unfortunately, this did not deter her father, who continuously and regularly abused her.

Eventually, Jo's short time of quiet acceptance ended. Diane was totally oblivious of this and had been worried about her little sister. Soon, Jo became her feisty self and Diane felt a degree of relief.

It took Jo a long time to tell Diane what their father had been doing to her. She didn't know what it was but felt it was wrong for some reason and felt ashamed, although she would not have been able to explain why or what he had been doing to her, somehow the little girl knew that it was something people did not talk about.

It would only be in later years, when they were young adults, that she would summon the courage to disclose what had happened to her.

# Chapter Seven

One night, the children were woken up suddenly by their dad urging them to get up and dress quietly. The children obediently got up, feeling drowsy and confused. When they got downstairs, they were told they were moving. Frank protested, "But it's in the middle of the night. Can't we move in the morning?" He earned a clip round the ear for his comment and was told to be quiet. Their parents had bagged up their few belongings and placed them in a wheelbarrow from the garden.

In the dark, cold night, the children trudged behind their parents in silence. They walked for what seemed ages to the children and approached the woods, walking through the woods was scary and Jo held Diane's hand. All the children wanted to ask where were they going and why but daren't in fear of provoking their parent's wrath.

Eventually, they stopped by a dilapidated caravan. "We're here, this is it." Francis announced, "This is our new home." He opened the door and they went into the cold, dank caravan with no lighting. He turned to Frank, "Where's your torch? Give it to me." Frank reluctantly gave his father his torch, which was his pride and joy and what he had been given as a present from Uncle Bertie. Fortunately, it was one of the few presents not taken by his parents to be sold as they didn't feel it would get them much money. Also, when they had the electricity switched off in the house, the torch was useful. Francis switched on the torch so they could see the caravan and told the children to go to bed.

Frank asked, "What? Where, Dad? Which room is mine?" Francis and Rita explored the caravan, there was only one bedroom. So, the boys were told to sleep outside under the caravan and given a blanket to share, Diane and Jo were given another blanket and told to lie on the floor whilst their parents took the only bedroom.

As they lay on the floor, Jo moaned, "I don't like it here."

Before Diane could response, Rita shouted, "Shut up, if I have to get out of this bed, you will be sorry, very sorry." Jo whimpered in fear and cuddled up to her sister. Diane took ages to sleep by the time she had soothed her younger sister.

Although the bed they had slept in at the house was lumpy and the mattress smelt of urine, it was more comfortable than the floor. Unfortunately, due to the smallness of the caravan, the girls would not have the refuge of a bedroom to escape to and would have to be very careful what they said, as it would be overheard by their parents.

In the morning, the family woke up later than usual due to their late-night walk to the caravan. The boys came into the caravan in the hope there would be some breakfast. Their parents were still in bed, asleep.

Frank looked through the cupboard to see if there was some food. But there was nothing. Diane got up and they both searched the meagre bags of belongings. She suddenly found a tin of powdered milk. Grabbing some spoons, they took turns in taking a spoonful of the powdered milk.

Diane asked, "What was it like sleeping outside?"

Frank grinned, "Bloody cold, that's what it was!"

Both John and Matthew repeated, "Bloody cold, bloody cold." The children giggled.

Diane looked nervously at the door to their parent's room, "Shush, you will wake them up." This was enough to keep her siblings quiet.

The caravan was in a place called Meadow Woods, with no neighbours and being in the forest, the family was cut off from the world. Over the next few weeks, the family became used to living in the cramped conditions in the caravan. A disadvantage was that they couldn't seek refuge in their bedroom. This was especially frightening as their father would be nasty if he had had a drink. When they lived in the house, they could hide in the basement or their room. Now, they had no escape from his wrath, except for going into the woods.

As the girls became older, they were able to recognise their father's change of mood when he had been drinking. So, they were able to go and hide somewhere in the house to escape his wrath. In the caravan, it was much worse. This one particular afternoon, the boys were out, looking for mushrooms and berries to pick for something to eat. Sometimes, they would go out of the forest and look for eggs to steal from the farmhouse. It was raining and Rita was out. Francis had just finished the fourth bottle of beer. He went to the cupboard and realised there were no more bottles left, he slammed the cupboard door in the kitchen area, making Jo jump with fright and muttered expletives. The girls were sat in the lounge part of the caravan. Francis slumped down in the chair, cupping his chin in his hand and stared at the girls, brooding. Diane immediately felt uncomfortable, she would not have been able to explain why, but knew that his mood had changed and they would be safer outside. She got up slowly and without a word grabbed Jo's hand, pulling her to her feet. Jo also sensed something was wrong and didn't say a word. As the girls started walking past him, he asked, "So, where are you going?" The girls froze with fright.

Diane quickly thought of something to say and said, "I need to go to the lavy (toilet)."

Francis regarded the girls, then muttered, "Alright." The girls rushed out of the caravan, only to find it was raining and there was no shelter, so they crawled underneath the caravan where the boys usually slept. Diane took the blanket and put it over herself and her sister.

Jo said, "I thought you wanted a wee?"

Diane looked at her, "Well, I don't. We had to get out cos Dad was getting funny."

Jo retorted, "You mean pissed, more like."

Diane wagged her finger at Jo, "Don't say that. It's not nice."

Jo jutted her chin, "Well, Frank says it." Diane raised her eyebrows, "Just cos our Frank says it don't mean you got to say it as well."

Despite her answering her older sister back, Jo was also learning to tell the signs of danger. Also, she feared as their mum wasn't in the caravan that Dad might take her into the bedroom and "do his nasty tricks" as she called it. Jo was a fiery little character, who loved her sister with all her heart, but she still couldn't bring herself to tell her sister about what their father did to her. Even if she felt she could tell her, she wouldn't have known how to say it as she didn't know what the words for it were. The two girls stayed under the caravan, wrapped up in the blanket, and eventually fell asleep.

Later, the boys came back pleased with their mission. They had managed to collect a tub full of blackberries, although judging by the number of purple stains on their mouths and clothes, they had eaten a fair share of the berries as well. They also managed to get some mushrooms and four eggs. They went into the caravan and saw the girls weren't there. Matthew went outside and crawled under the caravan to find two sleeping girls. He called out to Frank, "They are down here."

Frank saw the girls sleeping peacefully and felt a wave of protection for them. He knew the reason they had hidden from their father. Frank had often borne the brunt of his father's temper and suffered many a beating. Momentarily, as he regarded them, he felt he should protect them more, for the moment he vowed he would do this. Unfortunately, he was only a young child himself and as much a victim as they were. Although being a boy and being older, he had found refuge hiding in the woods when he knew his parents were becoming angry. Also, since being the finder of food sources, he was getting a little bit of appreciation from his feckless parents who should have been providing him and his siblings with food, shelter and love.

He woke the girls gently, and as Jo rubbed her eyes, he said, "Come in. We are all back except Mum. We have picked tons of berries, come and have some before that greedy bugger Matthew eats them all." Without hesitation, both girls grinned at the thought of something to eat, as they were starving and had not eaten all day. They both enjoyed the berries and stuck out their tongues to compare who had the blackest tongue. Even the resulting tummy ache after eating too many didn't worry them as they were just pleased to have had some food.

# Chapter Eight

School for the girls was a mixed blessing. On the one hand, they were in a clean, warm and organised environment. If it had not been for the other children teasing them, it would have been much better. They were not the only children who were teased. There were other children who were teased for different reasons. So, they weren't alone in that respect.

Occasionally, Frank would defend his sisters in a playground altercation, but a lot of the time, he was off running around and getting up to mischief with boys his own age. Although he felt a little protective of the girls, he didn't want to tarnish his reputation of being a 'daredevil' with the others. Therefore, he didn't encourage the girls to hang around with him and often told them to 'bugger off'.

Diane enjoyed school and had made friends quite easily, mainly due to her placid and caring nature. She had also made a good impression on the teacher who recognised Diane as being helpful in class and eager to learn. She loved reading as well and seemed to absorb knowledge easily. Diane tried not to get embroiled in fights or arguments at school. There was enough fighting and arguing at home. Diane liked the fact that the school day was structured and she knew what to expect in class. Although the teacher sometimes caned some of the naughtier children, Diane was always well behaved and didn't incur any wrath. The organised nature of the class made her feel safe. Diane enjoyed English and reading. The influence of Uncle Bertie's storytelling had fired her imagination. When she learnt to read, she found a world where she could escape from the neglect, abuse and poverty that was her lot in life.

Unfortunately, Jo struggled with school. She found reading difficult and seemed to struggle to read what the teacher put on the blackboard. Eventually, it was discovered that her eyesight was poor and the teacher sent home a note to her parents to get her eyes tested with an optician.

Of course, this never happened.

Jo also found herself in arguments and fights when other pupils teased the girls about their clothes or when they had nits. Jo would hit out and shout at the offending children. If Diane was there, she would pull her back and try to stop her little sister. Diane didn't want to be involved in arguments and fights, as there was enough shouting and violence at home. Due to her experiences at home, Diane learnt to keep quiet, but although she was quiet, she was assessing the person and the situation. However, Jo was more impulsive and would lash out with her tongue and sometimes her fists.

Constant hunger didn't help with either of the girls' learning. It was hard to concentrate on learning with the feelings of hunger and tiredness. Diane would comfort herself in the thought that Uncle Bertie and Aunt Bet would visit them. Both girls cherished those visits. For Jo, it was more difficult to think of this. Due to her nature, she was more a 'here and now' person and acted accordingly.

One day, the girls were going home from school together when Larry, an eight-year-old boy in their school, started calling them names and ridiculing their clothes. Diane had on a jumper that was becoming threadbare and was once her brother's and was too big. She also wore a skirt which was faded and dull. Jo was wearing a cardigan which was too small. She was five and was wearing a cardigan for a three-year-old. Both girls were thin and small for their age. Due to malnourishment, Jo had rickets and was often teased about that as well. Larry was calling out names and trying to ridicule the girls. A crowd of other children of various ages were looking on. No one thought to intervene even though Larry was twice the girl's size. They just thought a fight was brewing and wanted to watch. Most of them were secretly relieved they weren't the ones being bullied.

As Larry shouted unkind taunts at the girls, Diane tried to walk on and ignore it and grabbed Jo's arm to get her to do the same. Jo couldn't ignore it; she was incensed and so angry. For her, life was hard enough with the constant abuse and neglect at home. Unfortunately, being a tiny girl, she couldn't do anything about what her parents did, but she was not going to allow this boy to taunt and tease her. After another bout of rude name-calling, Jo shouted at Larry to stop. He laughed and pulled at her cardigan, "Where did you get this, in the dustbin?"

Jo became angry and pushed his hand away. He slapped her and she slapped him. He went to hit her again and she kicked his shins. Howling with anger and pain, Larry backed off. Diane grabbed Jo's hand and pulled her away. The crowd of children dispersed as the fight was over. As Diane urged Jo to come away, Jo shouted at him to leave them alone or she would kick him again. Once they were safely away from Larry, Diane let Jo's hand go. Diane tried to reason with Jo about fighting and that she should have ignored him. Jo jutted her chin at Diane, "Well, I sorted the bugger out. He won't come near us again."

Diane shook her head, "Don't say bugger, it's rude."

Jo grinned at her sister, "Okay, but if he hits me again, I will kick him." Diane knew that's just what Jo would do as well and felt slightly in awe of Jo's bravery.

Both sisters loved each other and were a source of comfort to one another. Although they were completely different in personalities, they were close. It was that bond that helped them stay strong and survive the abusive and unpredictable life they had at home.

When the sisters got home that afternoon, their mother was the only person in the caravan. She had sent the boys out to find out some food as the cupboard was bare. Their dad was at work and it was three days until payday and they had no money left.

Diane had to give her parents the note from the teacher about Jo needing to go to the opticians as it was suspected she needed glasses.

Diane knew if Jo gave her mum the note there would be a negative response. Their mother tried not to acknowledge Jo at all if possible, which was really distressing and confusing for the little girl, but it would be worse if she had her mother's attention, as that would result in a beating of sorts. Diane regarded her mother, trying to assess if it was safe to pass on the note, or would that cause her mother to become angry. The fact that Rita didn't appear to have had a drink and seemed relatively calm gave Diane the impression it would be safe to talk to her about it. "Err, Mum."

Rita looked at Diane, "What?"

Diane proffered the note in her mother's direction. "Teacher sent a note to you, about Jo."

Rita turned and looked at the girls, "What's she done now?"

Diane stepped back a little way from her mother. "Jo's not done anything wrong. The teacher gave us a letter cos Jo needs glasses." Rita snatched the note impatiently and read it.

Rita muttered to herself, "We haven't got money for bread and they want me to buy glasses for her. Bloody school, always interfering in our business." Rita then put the note down. She glared at the girls, "Well...go on go and get some water don't just stand there, get the bucket and go."

Diane picked up the bucket and called Jo to come with her. Jo followed her sister crossly. When they left the caravan, she grumbled, "Why do we have to get the water? We've been at school all bloody day."

Diane turned and shushed her sister, "Shush, be quiet. She will hear you."

Jo jutted out her chin defiantly, "I don't bloody care."

Diane rolled her eyes, "You will if you get a backhander or dragged into the cupboard, and don't say bloody, it's not nice."

Not wanting her sister to get the last word in, Jo responded, "Well, Mum and Dad do swear." Diane shook her head, thinking she had the most obstinate sister in the world, but for all that, she loved her.

Even at their tender ages, the girls were expected to work hard at home by getting fresh water to drink as there was no running water in the caravan. The bucket was heavy when filled so it took both girls together to carry it. But what was even more repulsive was when they were made to empty what they called the 'pee bucket'. The caravan didn't have a toilet so they used a bucket to wee in at night. Again, it was the girls who had to do this and they both hated it.

Their father would become particularly nasty after having too much alcohol to drink. Frank had learnt long ago to keep out of the way when their father was drunk. Diane was learning to read the signs and would try and keep herself and Jo out of his way when he was like this. However, this was difficult within the close confines of the caravan. One night, Francis was in the living area and was in a particularly unpleasant mood. It was a wintery night, dark and raining. At 9 pm, he decided that the girls should go out and empty the pee bucket. As the family never had a routine, the girls didn't have a bedtime as such. When they lived in the house, they were able to retreat into their bedroom if Diane sensed the atmosphere in the living area was becoming nasty. She would retreat to their room with Jo to get out of the way. Unfortunately, in the caravan, there was just one living area plus their parent's bedroom.

Due to his darkening mood and the erratic mood swings which followed his drinking alcohol, Diane got up immediately to see to the task. Jo was less willing and started to protest, "But, Dad, it's dark and…"

Her father turned to her and pushed his face close to hers and shouted, "You will bloody do as you are told, or you will get this!" He raised his fist threateningly over the little girl. Jo trembled and gulped with fright. Their father sat back down again and glared at the girls. Diane took Jo's hand and they went to empty the bucket. They carefully carried it between them, although it wasn't heavy, Diane didn't want to risk spilling anything. Both wrinkled their noses at the smell and the unpleasant task they had to carry out. As they walked out of the door, their father shouted, "And don't just chuck it out of the door, throw it further down away from the caravan." The girls carefully walked down the steps of the caravan and Diane closed the door. Outside it was pitch black and difficult to negotiate the steps with the bucket. It was pouring with rain and windy. "I'm cold." Jo whined, "Why can't he empty the bucket, the lazy sod?" Diane giggled, that was usually what their mum said to Dad and didn't correct her irrepressible sister.

The girls stopped for a minute. The bucket was heavy and smelly, they shivered, it was really cold and they weren't dressed for the weather.

They picked up the bucket and carried on struggling with it towards the woods. "I'm scared, it's spooky here. Do you think that ghost is out in the woods that Frank told us about?" Diane had to think quickly, sometimes their brother would tell his siblings stories. He was good at stories but sometimes too good and would scare both girls witless. The children didn't have books or any other source of entertainment and were left to entertain themselves. Frank had often listened to Uncle Bertie's stories and liked to embellish them. Being a mischievous boy, he took great delight in scaring his sisters. For him, it was another way to escaping the misery, abuse and poverty that was their lot. So, thinking fast, Diane declared that it was too wet for the ghost to be out and there was no need to worry. Jo sighed with relief, but then complained it was so scary. Ever the sensible one, Diane explained that the wood was the same as it was in the daytime, it just looked different in the night-time and the sooner they emptied the bucket, the sooner they could get back into the caravan. Diane wondered what was the lesser evil, being out in the cold, rainy wood or facing the storm in the caravan?

Neither girl liked the dark but Jo was especially frightened due to her being dragged by the hair into the dark cupboard.

Finally, they reached the neck of the woods and poured the offending urine out in the woods. Now that the bucket wasn't so heavy, Diane took Jo's cold hand; she could feel her sister shaking with fright. Without saying anything to Jo, Diane felt a wave of resentment and anger in her being.

What sort of parents let two tiny girls out to do such a job? Why couldn't they have parents who were like Uncle Bertie and Aunt Bet?

Jo was whimpering on the way back with fear and cold. When they got back into the caravan, to their relief, their dad had gone to bed, leaving the caravan in darkness. The two soaked children took off their dresses and Diane found their nightclothes, which was two old flannelette nighties that they had got for Christmas a year ago from their aunt and uncle. Having dried themselves with an old towel, they put on the nighties and settled down. Jo was still shaking and whimpering, Diane offered to tell her a story. "Jo, shall I tell you a story I made up?"

Jo sniffed, "Yes, can you tell me a nice story?" So, Diane told Jo a story about how they were both rescued by Aunt Bet and Uncle Bertie, how they were clean and wore nice clothes and ate properly. Both of the girl's tummies rumbled at the thought of eating something nice. For a short while, Diane transported both girls out of the misery that was their lives.

# Chapter Nine

The spring and summer months were the best for the family, giving them respite from the cold, harsh winters. Along with the better weather came the opportunity to go fruit picking. The children would be sent out and made to miss school in order to get mushroom, potato or fruit picking for their parents. Any money had to be handed over to their mother and the children never saw any of the benefits from this; the money would be spent in the pub. The only advantage for the children was the parents were out of the way for a while and they would play and be children.

The children often missed school in order to go fruit picking. The work was boring and arduous but they daren't shirk the responsibility as it was expected they would bring enough money back. The only advantage was that they also managed to eat a lot of fruit. One day, they were picking strawberries. All the children enjoyed the sweet succulent taste and ate a lot of them. Unfortunately, the girls ate so many that they didn't bring back much money. On their way home, Diane admitted she was worried, "Our mum's going to kill us. We haven't made a lot of money."

Both girls were feeling a little nauseous. Matthew was walking with them and not the least bit sympathetic, "I told you both you will get a bad belly eating as many as you did."

Jo jutted out her chin in defiance, "I ain't got a bad belly, so there…" then doubled up in pain.

Matthew laughed, "You will both get a bad earhole too when Mum sees you ain't picked any for her glasses of whiskey tonight." Both Jo and Diane looked worried.

When they got home, as predicted by their brother, their mother was not impressed. She frowned as the girls handed over the money, "Hmm, looks like we are a bit short here. Any reason why?" The girls stood in silence, shaking with fear, Rita had her hand on her hip and tapped her foot, "Well, I'm waiting. How come Matthew brought more money than you?"

Diane looked up, "Well, see, Mum, there weren't many strawberries. The farmer said it's a bad season for them."

Rita glared at the cowering girls, not an ounce of pity in her being as they cowered with their faces to the floor. Rita could see the tell-tale red around the girl's mouths showing they had eaten quite a lot of the strawberries and the anger surged within her body, "Bad season, bad season. You'll have to come up with better than that, my girl." Then, without warning, she dragged the two little girls by their hair and threw them into the cupboard.

Both girls rubbed their sore heads. Jo sniffed, "I hate her."

Diane replied, "Don't say that. She is our mum after all."

Jo jutted out her chin, "Don't mean I have to like her." Diane didn't argue, there was no point when Jo was like this. Diane felt the same but didn't verbalise it. At all costs, Diane tried to keep the peace, but Jo was right. Jo was still crying; she hated the dark and being shut in the cupboard. It didn't help that Matthew told them scary stories about the rats in the cupboard. But that was in the house. The tiny cupboard in the caravan was much smaller.

"Don't worry Jo. This cupboard is too tiny to have any rats in it. Now let me tell you a story." Diane was good at making up stories and had a good imagination. She liked to imagine what it would be like if they were rescued by Aunt Bet and Uncle Bertie. Sometimes, she told Jo the stories Uncle Bertie would tell them. Other times, she would make up what it would be like to go and live with them. This time, it was a story about them being adopted by their aunt and uncle. Diane told a lovely story about how they would have nice clothes and wear ribbons and eat nice food.

Jo looked up, "But not strawberries, Diane. I can't eat another strawberry ever again." Both girls giggled but knew that they would be tempted by the strawberries again.

Knowing hunger and deprivation as they did, any food they could get hold of, they would eat.

The girls did learn from the unfortunate experience and in order to keep themselves fed and also keep their parents happy, they would pick fruit quickly and efficiently to ensure that both parties were happy, their parents in the money they earned, and themselves having enough fruit to eat.

Apple picking was trickier; Frank was able to climb trees well and would shake the branches for the girls to catch the apples in and avoid them dropping on the ground and getting bruised, Unfortunately, if they fell to the ground, they bruised and then they would not be able to sell them. The children also went potato and mushroom picking, but this didn't have the sweet rewards that fruit had, so they found the task arduous and boring.

No matter how impoverished they were, their parents nearly always had some type of alcohol in the caravan whether it was from the pub, off licence or some homebrew given by a friend. In fact, on the occasions there were no alcohol to drink and their parents didn't have money to go out, this was sometimes worse than if they went out. The atmosphere would be tense and then their parents would bicker about whose fault it was that they didn't have anything to drink.

Diane and Jo would stay silent, sitting on the floor motionless, for they didn't want their parent's anger to be directed towards them. Diane would try and keep Jo quiet as Jo was impulsive and likely to say something. Even in the cold, icy winter, the girls would envy their brothers who were outside and out of the firing range.

Since moving into the dilapidated caravan in the woods, Diane sometimes likened their lives as being dark like the woods. She had a vivid imagination and would wonder what it was like to be rescued and saved from the woods. Although the woods seemed pleasant enough on a summer's day, in winter and at night they seemed dark and full of foreboding and menacing. What the little girl didn't realise was that it wasn't whatever was in the woods she needed to be wary of but what was in their caravan. She would daydream sometimes, wondering what it would be like to be rescued. If you had asked who would rescue them, it would always be Uncle Bertie and Aunt Bet.

Soon, the girls heard the heavy snoring coming from their parents' room.

It was now safe to whisper. Both girls snuggled up to keep warm. Jo asked, "Diane, what's Aunt Bet's house like?" whilst placing an icy-cold foot on Diane's leg.

"Get your foot off, its freezing. You know what it's like, you have been there before."

Jo moved her foot, "It was a long time ago, I can't remember."

Diane agreed, "I know, I wish we could go back and visit them again."

Jo nodded, "Me too," then said loudly, "I want cake."

Diane nudged her sister, "Shhhh, you will wake them and then we will get it."

Jo looked puzzled, "Get what, Diane?"

Diane frowned at her sister, "Well, it won't be cake, I can tell you that much. Now, go to sleep."

# Chapter Ten

For many families, Christmas is a time of goodwill, getting together with friends and family, enjoying a hearty meal and presents and enjoying the festive season. These moments, shared together, are the basis of fond memories, family jokes and traditions shared within that family.

Unfortunately, for the children, this was not the case. They never had a tree, presents or good food to eat at Christmas. None of the children had ever seen a Christmas cracker and would not know what it was.

For them, it was just like another day, but with the knowledge that most of their school friends would be enjoying time with their families, good food and nice presents.

The vast differences in their lives, compared to other children became more apparent when Diane started school. Diane was in awe of the huge Christmas tree in school with its gaily, bright baubles and tinsel. The tree was beautiful and she could not stop staring at it. The school was doing a Christmas nativity play and the teacher had picked Diane as one of the angels. With her blonde hair, the teacher thought she would look perfect. She sent Diane home with a note asking for her to be dressed as an angel in a sheet for a dress and silver tinsel for a halo. Diane was excited and rushed home to ask her mum to make the costume. She was momentarily caught up in the feeling of goodwill and excitement. Once home, she handed her mother the note and realised it was a mistake. As Rita read the note, she was swaying and Diane knew she was drunk. Rita held up the note and blinked at it, she was drunk again and could not focus on the words.

Diane said to her mother, "I'm going to be an angel and need a white sheet to make into a dress. Miss Cooper said she will make it if you give me a white sheet." Rita looked at the little expectant face looking up at her. Most parents would smile and their heart would melt with pride. They might even find their eyes filling with tears of joy, but not Rita.

"So where, missy, do you think we will find a white sheet then? Most of the sheets are piss stained because of that brother of yours. Where does Miss La Di Da Cooper think I got time to look for sheets?" Diane cowered in fear as Rita continued to read the note. "Tinsel, tinsel? Where the bloody hell does she think we got money for tinsel? We haven't even got a bloody Christmas tree anyway, so why would we have tinsel? These teachers have got a bloody nerve." Rita screwed up the note and threw it on to the floor and stormed out.

Diane stood motionless, feeling slightly angry with herself. Jo was standing by and had watched the scene and was sad for her sister. Jo didn't know much about Christmas. She went over to Diane and took her hand asking, "What's tinsel, Diane, can you eat it?"

Diane managed to raise a little smile, "No, silly, you put it on a Christmas tree."

Jo frowned, "What's a Christmas tree, is it like a conker tree?"

Diane told Jo about the Christmas tree at school and how magical it looked with the baubles, tinsel and lights. Jo had been ill, so had missed a couple of weeks from school. It had been a miserable time for her staying at home with a mother who didn't care and she missed Diane sorely. Jo had spent most of the time with her needs unattended. There had been no hot drinks or a mother to soothe her whilst she felt ill. The little girl spent most of the time trying to keep out of her mother's way, including retreat underneath the caravan where the boys slept.

Diane explained that you put presents under the tree. Jo put her head to one side and frowned, "What's presents, Diane?"

Diane explained it was like the presents of toys and clothes they got from Aunt Bet and Uncle Bertie, finishing with, "You know when they bring us stuff?"

Jo nodded, "Oh, the presents that turn into beer and whiskey?"

Diane frowned, "What do you mean?"

Jo said, "You know. When Aunt Bet and Uncle Bertie leave, they take the presents away and sell them for booze."

Diane sighed, "Yes, that's it." Diane wondered what it would be like to actually keep a toy or outfit they had been brought. Poor Aunt Bet and Uncle Bertie would buy them lovely dresses and matching ribbons, but apart from trying them on to show the outfits off to their aunt and uncle, most of the clothes never touched their backs again. Occasionally, they might get to keep a cardigan or underwear, but anything more expensive like a dress or coat would be gone.

Diane had to go to school the next day and admit to her teacher that there were no white sheets or tinsel. Fortunately, the teacher managed to get some material and Diane was an angel in the play, but there were no doting parents to watch her perform and no-one to tell her how well she had done, apart from the teacher. After the play, the parents congratulated their children on how well they had done and how proud they were of them. Diane fought back tears of sadness as this occasion, where everyone was supposed to be so kind and nice to each other, illustrated just how different her life was. Her only consolation was that the performers had warm mince pies to eat and her teacher let her have a couple of mince pies to bring home to share with Jo.

The other matter confusing Diane was about Father Christmas, in the five Christmases she had experienced, there had never been any sign of this jolly, fat man in a red suit. There were no presents, no tree or anything to indicate that Christmas was in their household. She talked to Jo about it. She talked about how her friends and said they put out mince pies, milk and a glass of sherry for Father Christmas when he came into the house to deliver the presents. Jo frowned, "Well, if we left a glass of sherry out for Father Christmas, our mum would drink it anyway! That's why we don't get anything."

Diane nodded gravely, "Yes, that's it, that's why we don't get presents."

Jo frowned, "Well, Father Christmas is a mean old bugger, not giving us nothing."

Diane shushed her up, she didn't want the all-seeing and all-hearing Father Christmas listening to Jo talking like this— just in case!

On the last day of school, they had a Christmas party. Diane's eyes widened at the array of delicious party food and she sneaked some sandwiches in her pockets as a lot of the children were eating the crisps and the cakes rather than the sandwiches, despite the teacher's plea of, "Children, please eat at least two sandwiches." Diane knew the food would be thrown out, so she felt she was doing them a favour. She managed to grab some biscuits too, *Jo would like these,* she thought, smiling to herself. It would make a change from the sugared water and stale bread which was their normal diet. In fact, to Diane, the sandwiches seemed quite exciting with butter and cheese or ham in them.

Diane looked at all the excited and merry faces of the other children and felt a pang, wondering why was their life so different? Since starting school, she had realised that other people's lives were so removed from her family's existence.

A lot of the other children in her class were given sweets regularly. After the restrictions of the Second World War and the rationing that went on for years after, society had come into a more affluent phase, but this seemed to bypass Diane and her family. Unfortunately, some of the girls who brought in sweets would share with each other, but it was rare that anyone shared with Diane or Jo because they never had any sweets to give back. Occasionally, they were lucky, and a kindly girl might give them a sweet each, but those occasions were few and far between. On an odd occasion that they tasted a sweet, they thought it was wonderful.

The longer she was at school, the more she realised their lives were different and it disturbed her. At school, all the children were encouraged to behave well, use their 'Ps' and 'Qs' and not swear. They were taught that bad things happened to naughty children. Diane didn't consider herself or Jo naughty and found it difficult to understand why they seemed to be constantly punished and lacking what most children in her class enjoyed.

She found it hard to join in conversations that the other girls had about what they were hoping Father Christmas would bring and she wondered if Father Christmas knew their address as he had not visited them ever. Diane wondered if there was a way to let Father Christmas know where they lived. From hearing some of the other children talk, she realised you had to go into the department store where Father Christmas was and see him and tell him what you wanted. Diane dismissed this idea as she knew you would need to get a bus to go into town and she never had any money.

Diane wistfully thought, "Perhaps he could bring them some presents; warm clothes, candy canes, a dolly for her and a new dolly bath for Jo as Jo had been so upset about losing her other dolly's bath." Diane considered that Father Christmas would have to give them things that her parents could not sell for alcohol. They never took Jo's bath, so that would be good for Jo to have that and perhaps if she had a dolly, she would cut the doll's hair a bit so it looked 'funny' and they could not sell it but she would still love the doll anyway. As for the sweets and chocolate, they could eat that before their mum and dad could sell it.

The other children in school were so excited to have the two week's holiday for Christmas; they put on their warm coats, hats and clothes; they chattered happily, talking about what they expected for Christmas, looking rosy-cheeked in the cold air and really excited. The snow had fallen the night before and as they left the school, the children happily threw snowballs at each other and shrieked with delight.

The other children had left the class and only Diane was still there.

Diane reluctantly put on her threadbare old coat which used to be her brother's and was handed down to her. She had no hat or gloves to wear. The teacher addressed her, "Come on, Diane. All the others have gone now. You need to go home and start enjoying Christmas. It's only two days until Christmas Eve." Diane looked at her teacher sadly; she was reluctant to leave the warm haven of the classroom. She had purposely avoided leaving with the other children as she didn't want to be in a snowball fight as there would be no warmed clothes or fire to sit around when she returned home freezing and wet.

Diane enjoyed school for she liked learning, especially reading, and knew she was safe. The school environment was comfortingly predictable and she knew what to expect and there were no sudden outbursts of shouting and hitting. In those days, the teachers could cane you if you misbehaved, but Diane never did anything to cause the teacher's wrath so she felt safe at school. The teacher looked at Diane and felt sad knowing that this child would not be waking up on Christmas day with wide, shining eyes in expectancy of presents and nice food. If she was lucky, she might avoid a beating and that would be it.

Diane looked sadly at her teacher, "Merry Christmas, Miss."

She turned to go and the teacher stopped her, "Wait, I have something for you." Diane turned and the teacher gave her a small bar of chocolate.

Diane looked at the chocolate bar. She rarely had chocolate and this was a real treat for her. For the first time that day, her eyes light up as she smiled. "Thanks, Miss."

The teacher smiled back, "Not a word to the other children as they will all want a bar of chocolate."

Diane grinned, "Okay, Miss, it's a secret." The teacher looked sad as her last student left the room. *I expect you have a lot of secrets, Diane,* she thought.

Diane wisely hid the bar of chocolate up her sleeve. She would save it for later. The girls only had chocolate when Aunt Bet and Uncle Bertie visited.

Diane decided to keep the chocolate bar hidden until Christmas Day, it would be a treat for her and Jo on Christmas night once the boys were outside asleep and their parents had gone to bed.

The day before Christmas Eve, Uncle Bertie and Aunt Bet arrived to give them presents. Although by now the girls knew it was unlikely they would keep the clothes and presents, there would be some sweets or chocolate which they would be able to keep. As soon as their aunt and uncle sat down, the girls bagged a lap each. Aunt Bet laughed to see the girls so excited. It was a change for the sounds of laughter to be coming from the caravan. Aunt Bet didn't ask why they didn't have a tree. She had done that in the past and it resulted in an awkward atmosphere with Rita snapping at her. Also, the caravan was tiny and there would be no room for a tree. Bet sensed something was not quite right with the family but had no idea of what was really happening. So, she tried to help by buying clothes and presents for the children. She had no idea that most of these items were sold. Aunt Bet passed a parcel each for Diane and Jo to open before Christmas. She had bought the girls a dress each. Diane's dress was a powder blue and white checked dress and matched her blonde hair beautifully. Jo had a similar dress in pink which complimented her dark brown hair. Both girls tried on the dresses and twirled around in them. Aunt Bet smiled at the girls kindly, thinking how pretty they looked. If only Rita would make more of an effort with their hair which always looked tangled and unwashed. However, Bet kept these thoughts to herself, it wouldn't do to upset Rita who was so volatile and might stop them from visiting the children. She handed the girls some matching ribbons which went with the dresses. Aunt Bet addressed the little girls, "Oh, you look lovely, girls. Don't they look pretty, Rita?"

Rita grimaced and said, "Yes," reluctantly. She was more interested in getting the clothes off their backs and selling them and the other presents, so she and Frank could go to the pub for a Christmas drink. The girls enjoyed wearing the new dresses and the new, clean smell which made a difference to the old, musty-smelling dresses they normally wore. Jo twirled in her dress and loved the way it billowed out and liked the newness of it. Jo grinned at her aunt and uncle, "When I'm rich, I will have hundreds of dresses." Diane and their aunt and uncle laughed. Jo's eyes sparkled and her face lit up, it was a change for the little girl to have positive attention and she loved it.

Suddenly, the cheeky smile Jo was sporting disappeared, as Rita came up to the girls, looking menacing as she bent over to talk to them. "Right, come on girls, take those lovely dresses off and we will put them away for Christmas Day." She addressed the girls sharply. Jo looked up, wondering if her mother meant they could keep the dresses and was about to say something when Diane nudged her and gave her a warning look. The girls reluctantly took off the pretty dresses and handed them to their mother whilst keeping the ribbons in their tightly clenched fists. Fortunately, Rita was too occupied with taking the dresses, she forgot to ask for the ribbons.

Although disappointed at the loss of the dresses which Diane knew they would never see again, they did enjoy a few hours with Aunt Bet and Uncle Bertie, they had brought a cake and insisted everyone have a slice. All the children enjoyed eating the cake as it had been the best thing they had eaten in a while. Although they occasionally ate cake when Frank sometimes earned a few pennies and would go to the baker for the stale bread and cakes which were cheaper. It was a change to eat a slice of cake that was fresh and light. Aunt Bet then handed each child a present wrapped gaily in Christmas paper. All too soon, their beloved uncle and aunt left as their parents were seeing them out, both went out with them to say goodbye and in the hope that Bet would give them some money. As they said goodbye, Francis pleaded poverty to his sister Bet, "You know it's so difficult with the kids they are always growing out of their clothes. So, if you could help out? We just want to make Christmas happy for our young ones," he asked hopefully. Bet, being kind-hearted, passed him a pound note. Francis grabbed it jubilantly before she could change her mind and gave her a peck on the cheek, "Thanks, Bet, I always say to the lads in the pub what a heart of gold you got." Bet frowned at him and he pocketed the pound note before she could ask for it back.

As soon as their relatives were out of earshot, Francis grinned happily and grabbed his coat and urged Rita to come to the pub with him. "Look, I've got the entrance fee."

Rita hurriedly got her coat and followed him as she wasn't going to miss out on a couple of drinks. "Wait for me," she commanded, "You're not spending all that on yourself, you greedy bugger."

Meanwhile, in the caravan, the girls wriggled with excitement, wondering what was in the presents. Even though their parents had gone, none of the children dared touch the presents, they knew they would get a beating if they did. Frank burst their bubble of excitement, "Dunno what you are getting all excited about, you know we can't keep the presents."

Diane sighed, "I know, I just wish they would buy something they didn't want to sell, like Jo's dolly bath that time." Diane looked at Jo, "Weren't the dresses pretty, Jo? I felt like a princess in mine."

Jo sighed "Yeh, but that's the last we will see of them dresses."

Diane opened up her hands, "We still have the ribbons though," and Jo grinned. Diane hid the ribbons in the hole of their pillow. Their mother never bothered tidying the makeshift bed they slept in so she knew it was safe.

Safe in the knowledge their parents were out of the way, the children played together and when it was time to go to bed, Jo begged Diane to tell a story. Diane had a good imagination and would tell her brothers and sister a story. She could transport them out of their misery into a world of adventure, fun and laughter. She always made the endings happy, perhaps in the hope that one day she could feel happy herself.

Christmas Day came and went, barely being acknowledged. The pretty dresses which the girls had tried on and the trousers and jumpers the boys had were packed up and sold before Christmas and in their place were bottles of beer, gin and whiskey. An onlooker gazing through the window would not have seen a typical family playing games, reading jokes on Christmas crackers and enjoying a hearty Christmas lunch. Instead, they would have seen several cold, unhappy, and hungry children whose parents were in their bedroom sleeping off what they had drunk earlier on.

When they could hear their parents snoring, the children knew it was a little safer to talk, although Diane warned them not to be loud as they didn't want to wake their mum and dad. Matthew found a pack of cards and they played snap. The boys began moaning about being hungry, they looked in the cupboard and there was still some of the cake Aunt Bet had brought the other day when they delivered the Christmas presents.

Matthew took out the cake and asked the others whether they should eat it. They were taking a chance because when their parents found out, they would all get a beating. He looked at Diane, "What do you think. Should we risk it?" Diane looked at the closed bedroom door where the snoring was coming from and narrowed her eyes. Suddenly, she recalled how the children in her class with their tales of trees, cakes, roast dinners and presents. Most of her friends at school would be tucking into a big meal followed by Christmas pudding and would be playing with their toys and would have a beautiful Christmas tree like the one in school. She felt a wave of resentment towards the two drunken parents who were sleeping off copious amounts of alcohol and felt angry. Not only did they not have a Christmas meal, but there was also hardly anything in the larder due to the actions of her feckless parents.

Diane nodded at Matthew, "Let's eat it. I will get a knife to cut it with."

Jo looked at her normally sensible and cautious sister, "But, Di, what about our mum? You will get a hiding if she finds out."

Diane looked at Jo, "Well, I'm hungry, we are all hungry."

Jo looked at Diane in astonishment, "But we will get a beating."

Diane nodded, "But we will still have had the cake."

Frank added, "With any luck, they will have been too boozed up to remember the cake. If they ask, we will say they ate the cake when they were drunk!" The others giggled whilst Diane cut the cake in more or less equal portions and the children ate their slice each.

"Merry Christmas." Diane grinned and they all giggled nervously. Diane washed the knife and then took out the cake stand and threw it away. "If Mum or Dad ask about the cake, we can tell them they ate it when they were drinking." Satisfied with this explanation, the children felt happier having eaten something and continued to play cards.

Later at bedtime, before they settled to sleep, Diane produced the bar of chocolate and snapped it in half and gave half to Jo, "Don't tell the boys. The bar is not that big so I saved it just for us." Jo smiled and her eyes lit up at the unexpected treat.

As she put a piece of chocolate in her mouth, she asked, "Di, tell me about the Christmas tree and what it looked like." As they savoured the chocolate pieces, Diane described the Christmas tree at school and how pretty the lights looked.

# Chapter Eleven

Life continued along the same way for the next year. The children barely went to school after Christmas. Sometimes, Diane yearned to be at school, as the classroom was warm and it was an escape from the deprivation and violence that home life brought. Unfortunately, as neither girl possessed a decent coat and their shoes were full of holes, they weren't able to walk to school in the bleak, icy winter conditions.

Despite the poor home conditions, the children carried on, trying to avoid beatings and generally survive and appreciate the odd occasions when things were pleasant, such as visits by their uncle and aunt. As the girls became older and went to school, they realised that their life differed to those of the children they sat in school with. For Diane, school had been a mixed blessing. She enjoyed learning and especially reading. Sometimes, the teacher would lend her a picture storybook, which she guarded zealously and hid from her parents.

In the playground, life was less easy. Diane had a few friends but tended to look out for Jo who was frequently getting into rows and fights with her peers. The outspoken and fiery little girl would shout at anyone who teased her, and despite Diane's advice, could not ignore the spiteful taunts. Jo didn't enjoy the lessons at school, she struggled to read as the glasses Aunt Bet had bought her had broken and their mother threatened to beat her if she told Aunt Bet. Both girls were often tired due to lack of food, and sometimes, lack of sleep when they would be woken by their parent's loud, alcohol-fuelled arguments, which would turn physical. The noise kept the children awake and they would be on high alert to avoid blows or being caught in the crossfire. For both girls, the constant hunger also impeded their learning as they found it hard to concentrate.

Although the family didn't have many visits from their relatives, apart from Uncle Bertie and Auntie Bet, they did have a cousin, Benny, who was in his late teens. Benny would visit and sometimes have a beer with their dad. Benny would make the children laugh and sometimes play fight with the older boys.

Recently, Rita had become more irritable than normal, and the physical arguments between her and Francis were more frequent. She would lose patience with the children and the shouting and beatings were happening more often.

One day, their cousin Benny popped into the caravan. He chatted over a beer and then both Benny and the parents went outside the caravan.

Diane watched out of the caravan window. She couldn't hear what they were saying but could see both parents were angry and there was a lot of arm-waving. The adults left without telling the children where they were going. Relieved to be free from the heavy, loaded atmosphere, the children went out of the caravan to play in the woods. A few hours later, they were outside the caravan and Benny turned up.

Benny spoke to the girls and told them to get some things as they were going on a 'holiday' to stay with Auntie Bet and Uncle Bertie. Benny smiled but it was a forced smile, the girls were too young to notice this. "Get your things then, and we will go," he urged, and kept looking around as if expecting someone to come in.

Diane looked up at him, "What things?"

Benny replied, "Nightie, spare clothes, toothbrush." Both girls picked up a dirty, washed-out nightie each.

Benny asked where their coats were. "Jo doesn't have a coat, just a cardi," Diane explained and grabbed the shabby coat she had and Jo's cardigan which was for a child aged three years but still fitted the little girl.

Benny looked at the girls, "Have you got everything?" They nodded. Benny looked at the lack of belongings and realised just how dire the situation was, it was almost as if he was seeing them for the first time. Not one of the children had a decent piece of clothing to their name. Benny jerked his head, "Come on, then."

As they walked through the forest, Diane asked, "But what about Mum and Dad? We didn't say goodbye." Benny explained that they knew the girls were going but were busy so asked him to take them to their aunt and uncle's house. Benny walked quickly and the girls struggled to catch up. He seemed to be in a hurry and didn't say much to them until they were out of the forest. The weather was freezing and the girls' legs were bare and frozen. Their flimsy shoes were soaked.

Later, they caught a bus and once they sat down, Jo asked, "What is a holiday?" Diane shrugged; she had heard of people talking about holidays at the seaside but didn't know what it was. Benny explained it was where you go for a break and reminded them they were staying with Bet and Bertie. Both girls were bemused. They had rarely been taken to see their aunt and uncle and could barely remember their house. They hadn't seen their aunt and uncle since Christmas which seemed a long way off.

A few hours later, they disembarked from the second bus. Both girls were tired. Benny had bought them an iced bun and drink, which was a rare treat, but they still felt hungry and cold. Only the thought of seeing their aunt and uncle cheered the little girls slightly. They were both tired, hungry and cold.

They arrived at Bet and Bertie's house. Once inside, the warmth enveloped the girls. They had forgotten how warm and cosy their house was as they rarely visited them. Auntie Bet greeted them warmly, giving them a hug and a kiss, "Where are your belongings?" she asked.

Jo looked up, "What are belongings?" Diane said that was all they had.

Aunt Bet looked confused, "No coat, no toilet bag or spare clothes."

Benny shook his head grimly, "This is all they have."

Uncle Bertie appeared, "Where are my girls?" The girls forgot how cold and tired they were and flew to him for a hug.

Diane then turned to her aunt and said, "Benny told us we are staying with you for a holiday."

Bet looked at Benny, who signalled for the girls to come to him. Looking at the two small girls, he swallowed hard, when he had their attention, he said grimly, "No, girls, I have brought you here to live with Auntie Bet and Uncle Bertie, because if I had not taken you away then they would have killed you."

Diane frowned, "They? Who are they?"

Benny replied, "Your mum and dad." Benny explained that when he came to collect them, their mother said, "Take them now, or I will kill them. I've had enough; I don't want them in my sight." Diane gasped and grabbed Jo's hand. Tears filled her eyes. Diane was astute enough to take in the enormity of this and felt hurt that her mother would say such things. Even though she had never shown them much love or tenderness, she was still their mum. The atmosphere in the room was charged. Auntie Bet shook her head at Benny as if to say he shouldn't have said that in front of the girls. Jo looked wide-eyed at her relatives, confused, the enormity of what had been said had not sunk in.

Taking charge, she ushered the girls to come and sit down whilst she made them something to eat for tea. Both girls looked puzzled, Jo asked, "Tea? What's that?"

Bet frowned, "Tea. You know you have breakfast in the morning before you go to school—"

Jo interrupted, "We don't have breakfast and don't go to school no more."

Bet looked shocked but continued, "Then you have dinner at lunchtime and then tea after school." Both girls still looked confused. Bet shook her head and spoke to Benny, "This is worse than I thought. They don't even know the names of mealtimes."

Benny rolled his eyes, "Aunt Bet, you wouldn't believe what went on there. Their mum and dad are drinking all the time. Those kids don't know what day of the week it is. They'd never seen a book till they went to school." Bet shook her head sadly. Benny continued, "They were going to poison them," jerking his head towards the girls. Bet motioned for him to lower his voice, she dreaded to think what Benny would say next and didn't want the girls to get even more frightened than they already were. Lowering his voice, Benny explained how Rita had become worse recently, he didn't know what the problem was but Frank had told him how she was losing her temper all the time, and that he had to intervene when she was assaulting Matthew and went too far. Benny went on to explain that the girls were no longer attending school, as Rita didn't want the authorities questioning her due to their lack of coats and decent shoes.

The girls sat side by side, still holding hands. Diane looked at Aunt Bet and Benny, wondering what they were talking about. What were these mealtimes they were speaking of, what were days of the week and what was poison? Diane could tell by the way the adults reacted that poison was a bad thing. She recalled one of her brother's friend had eaten some poisoned berries and had a bad belly, so it must be dangerous.

They looked around the room which was nicely furnished and seemed so much more comforting than their home. The fire was blazing and looked welcoming and warm. Although, following the incident with the toy bath, Jo was wary of fires and never got too close to one. Uncle Bertie chatted to them, trying to make them feel welcome and at home.

Presently, Aunt Bet came in with some cheese sandwiches on a plate for each of them. She handed each girl a plate. Both girls stared at the sandwiches. "Go on, eat up girls," their aunt urged them. She went back into the kitchen and came out with a plate of sandwiches for Benny. She glanced at the girls who had not touched their sandwiches. Bet whispered to Benny, "Why aren't they eating? They looked half-starved."

Benny explained, in a low voice, that one of the ways their father 'teased' the girls was to hand them some food, then take it and if they tried to eat the food, would grab it back, eating it himself. Benny continued, "See, when they were drunk, they thought it was a joke."

Aunt Bet bristled with annoyance, tutting, "To tease the poor little mites like that. What sort of parents are they? I'm ashamed of my brother, I really am." At this stage, Bet didn't know the half of what had happened to the children. She guessed that Rita did 'put on a show' but didn't realise the extent of the neglect and abuse that the girls had suffered at their parents' hands. Bet walked over to the girls who were still holding their plates with the uneaten sandwiches on them. "Go on, eat up now, girls. I won't take the food away. We don't want it to go to waste now, do we?"

Diane looked up, "Really, we can eat them, Aunt Bet, can we?" Aunt Bet nodded and had to turn quickly as she didn't want the girls to see the tears in her eyes.

Diane cautiously picked up her sandwich and took a bite, Jo watched, waiting for Aunt Bet or Benny to take the food, but they didn't. Diane nodded at her little sister to eat as well. It was only a cheese sandwich, nothing adventurous or special, but to the girls, that sandwich tasted wonderful. As the girls ate, Bet turned to Bertie, "I will have to give them a bath and get the nit comb in their hair. Both heads are full of lice." Bertie nodded in agreement.

Benny got up and finished his cup of tea, "Well, I'd better be off now, Auntie and Uncle."

Bet stood up, "Thank you for bringing them, poor little mites." She then lowered her voice, "Is it really that bad?"

Benny replied quietly, "Yeh, and worse. She's really losing it, Auntie. She laid into Jo something chronic for no reason at all. It would only be a matter of time and one of them would have ended up being dead." Benny turned to the girls, "Now, you two be good for your Auntie Bet. I'm off now, bye." The girls muttered goodbye then looked at each other. It was one of the rare times in their life that they were alone with their aunt and uncle without a sibling or parent with them. They didn't know what to expect. Were their aunt and uncle really as kind as they always thought they were? Or were they 'putting on a show' as their older brother often said about their own parents when anyone 'official' knocked on the door.

Aunt Bet brought them out of their thoughts by asking if they wanted an apple. Both girls nodded. She brought them apples and they ate them quickly as if fearing the apple would be taken away. Bet, then, gave both girls a mug of hot milk. After they had eaten, Bet decided it was time to give them a bath and put them to bed.

In the bathroom, both girls had taken off their clothes. Bet looked at the two thin bodies, both of which were covered in scratches, bites and various degrees of bruising. Both girls were grubby with tide marks on their arms and legs. It was obvious that they had just had a wet flannel administered to the parts of their arms and legs that showed. Bet's eyes filled with tears, "This was never right, the poor little mites."

Once the bath had water in, Bet tested it wasn't too hot and told the girls to climb in. Jo looked at Diane and both were fearful, since living in the caravan, they had not had a proper bath and it looked scary with the steam coming off the water. After some persuasion, Diane climbed in very cautiously. But Jo refused, "I ain't getting in there!" Bet tried to persuade her and tried to lift her into the bath, but Jo screamed and struggled. Bet was at a loss at what to do, her shock at finding out their parents were planning to kill the girls, the sudden rescue by Benny, and then seeing the stark reality of how deprived, abused and neglected the girls were had upset and worried her. She lost her patience and slapped Jo smartly twice on the legs, demanding her to get into the bath. Jo obediently climbed into the bath, giving Bet a mutinous look.

Fresh and clean from their bath, both of the girls felt better. "Can we have another bath, Auntie Bet?" asked Jo, who had clearly changed her mind and felt a bath was a good experience.

Bet smiled, "Of course you can, you can have another bath tomorrow." Bet already had some nightdresses for the girls which she had bought for their ages as Benny had spoken to her a week before and she agreed to take on the girls. Both nighties were far too big. Bet would ask her friend to take them up for her. The girls liked the smell and feel of the new nighties. The next hurdle for Bet was delousing their hair. The girls patiently allowed her to use the smelling lotion on their heads and sat quietly as she combed with the nit comb. Once done, their hair was washed and dried. Clearly satisfied this job was done, Bet explained to the girls that the nits would be gone and they wouldn't need to scratch their heads again.

Jo grinned, "They can't call us Nitty Noras at school anymore now, can they, Diane?"

Once the lotion was rinsed off and their hair was dry, it was time for bed.

Diane looked at Jo, "Your hair is really shiny." Jo smiled, enjoying some rare praise. Diane was right, Jo's brunette hair shone beautifully, as did Diane's own blonde hair. Aunt Bet encouraged them both to brush their hair. Before that, their hair would have been lank and greasy from lack of washing and it was very rare for them to have a proper hair wash unless they had visitors.

The girls were tired by now and Bet asked what time did they normally go to bed. Jo looked at Diane who shrugged. The girls had never had a proper routine for bedtime or meals. They couldn't tell the time and the family had never had a clock in the caravan. Bet decided 7.30 pm was late enough for the girls and told them to say goodnight to Uncle Bertie and took them upstairs to their room. Their room was neat and tidy with two beds with matching eiderdowns. The girls had a bed each and chose which bed they would sleep in. Bet had thoughtfully bought both girls a teddy bear which was placed on each bed.

Aunt Bet kissed them goodnight on the cheek, switched out the light and closed the door. Minutes later, Jo said, "It's nice having a warm bed to ourselves, innit Di?"

Diane was really tired and replied with an, "Mmm yes."

Jo continued, "Yeh, it's nice and comfy and the sheets don't smell of piss."

Diane sat up, "Don't swear, its rude, Jo."

Jo jerked her chin defiantly, "Least I don't have to share with you now."

Diane replied, "At least I'm not sharing with you. So there."

Ten minutes later, Diane was about to drift into sleep and Jo had got out of her bed and tapped her, "Can I share with you? My bed's too big?"

Diane sighed, pulling back the bed covers, "Oh come on then."

Half an hour later, both girls were curled up in Diane's bed, fast asleep in each other's arms. When Bet went to check on them, she told Bertie. "They have a nice bed each and they are sharing the one bed," Bertie suggested they were used to sleeping that way and being in a new place would seem strange to them. Bet nodded, "Once they get used to living here, I'm sure they will sleep in separate beds."

It took several weeks of talking and cajoling the girls to sleep in their own beds. Ever since they were babies, they had slept in the same bed and comforted each other when the other had been hurt or when both of them were scared about what was happening.

It was several weeks later when both girls felt secure enough to sleep in her own bed. Occasionally, if one of the girls was upset or suffered a flashback, they would revert to sharing a bed, but most of the time they slept separately.

# Chapter Twelve

The girls had been living with their aunt and uncle for a couple of weeks. They were beginning to adapt to their new life and enjoyed having regular meals. A new experience for them was learning to take pride in their appearance. Their aunt encouraged good hygiene, baths, brushing teeth and hair. When the girls first came to live with their aunt and uncle, they were skinny, very pale, spotty, had greasy hair and lacked energy. A good diet and routine changed that. Both began to start to look and feel healthier.

However, Bet was worried about Jo's legs which didn't look right. So, she took her to the GP. The GP examined the little girl and turned to Bet saying, "This child has rickets. How did she get to such a state?" The GP explained rickets were due to malnutrition. Bet was taken aback and shocked. The GP looked stern and this upset Bet as she felt he thought Jo's condition was due to her.

Before Bet could compose herself and explain, Jo exclaimed, "Her didn't give me them ric things. It was cos of me mum and dad. They didn't bloody feed us proper!" Bet shushed Jo but was secretly relieved that Jo had butted in, and as a result, the GP's attitude changed dramatically when Bet went on to explain that the girls were no longer with their parents and living with them. The doctor gave Bet advice on what kind of diet was needed. Later, with a good diet, Jo's condition improved and she no longer had rickets.

Bet had contacted the Social Services office and explained the situation and it was agreed they could become foster carers for the girls.

As Bertie was blind and Bet was partially sighted, the family were assigned a child care worker (now known as a social worker).

The following week, their worker visited the family. Her name was Amanda James. She explained to the girls that their aunt and uncle would look after them in future and they would remain in Bristol. "We won't go back to our mum and dad?" Diane asked.

Amanda smiled gently at the serious look on Diane's face. "Do you like living with your auntie and uncle?" she asked the girls. Both girls grinned and nodded emphatically. She asked them did they want to live with their aunt and uncle and both said yes. She then asked if they would like to go back to live with their birth parents.

Before Diane could say anything, Jo shouted, "Hell no!"

Before anyone could say anything, Bertie appeared to be choking. Amanda and the girls looked concerned and Diane rushed up to him, "Are you alright, Uncle Bertie?"

Bet looked up, "He's okay." She knew that this was Bertie's way of disguising his laughter and vowed she would have a chat with him later. By now, she knew Jo had some choice language which she was determined would stop, and Bertie laughing would only encourage her all the more.

Bet was shocked that the girls didn't know names of meals, what a clock was or even being aware of a washing routine. One night the girls were bathed and in their nighties, Bet picked up the discarded clothes the girls had worn that day. The girls looked alarmed, Diane asked, "Where are you taking our clothes?"

Jo more defiantly said, "Give us back our clothes." Bet shook her head and explained she was taking the clothes to wash them and when they were cleaned, she would put them in the drawers. Jo folded her arms, "Don't believe you."

Bet showed the girls the chest of drawers with the neatly folded pants, vests and cardigans and then the wardrobe which held their dresses and skirts. "See, you both have plenty of clothes to wear, but once they have got dirty or been worn, they need to be washed and ironed."

After being with their aunt and uncle for around three weeks, the girls had their first day at school. Aunt Bet had bought some pinafore dresses and tops for school. The girls were nervous about their first day at school. Diane remembered being bullied for not having proper clothes and feeling inferior to the other girls who wore nice clothes and had nice ribbons. With their parents, the girls rarely had ribbons, only ones that Aunt Bet would bring. But eventually, they would be lost. Bet looked at the girls in their new clothes looking smart. "You both look very tidy and smart, all set for school."

Bertie then said, "But there's something missing. Girls, come and see what's in my hands." Both girls ran to him and each opened a clenched hand which revealed ribbons. Blue for Diane and red for Jo. Bet put the ribbons in their ponytails which were done up with a bobble.

When the girls looked at themselves in the mirror Bet guided them to, Jo exclaimed in surprise, "Who're those girls staring at us?"

Diane giggled and nudged her, "It's us, silly. We are looking in a mirror." Jo frowned, looking confused. They hadn't had a mirror at their home in the caravan, the only mirror they had was a compact mirror their mother had when doing her makeup. Diane swelled with pride, "We look smart now, Jo. None of those kids can make fun of us now."

Jo nodded, "Yeh, and if they do, I'll hit them," and bared her fist.

Bet shook her head, "No, we won't have any talk like that here, young lady. You are going to school and will do as you are told." Then, addressing Jo, "Especially you, young lady. You need to mind your manners and none of that bad language either."

Aunt Bet looked stern as if she meant it, but Diane noticed a twinkle in her eye. "We will be good, Aunt Bet. I promise."

Bet walked them to school on the first day so they knew the way.

When she said goodbye to the girls, she said, "Now have a good day at school. You listen to the teachers and behave."

Diane looked serious and nodded, "We will, Aunt Bet." Jo didn't look too sure. Bet took them to their teachers before leaving them. When Jo realised, she was going into a different class from Diane, she panicked. Although Diane had gone to school when they lived with their parents, it was not often.

Jo initially refused to go with her teacher, Miss Tibbs. "Come on, Joanna," the teacher held out her hand to Jo, "Come with me."

Jo pouted, "Don't wanna. I want to stay with Diane," and with that, clung to Diane, sobbing.

After a while, Jo was persuaded to release Diane and go with her teacher. "I will see you in the playground at break time, Jo. Be good."

Diane was aware of the other pupils watching her curiously, as they did with all new pupils. They sat her at a desk with a girl called Lisa who smiled at her. Lisa had brown curly hair which seemed to take on a life of its own and a freckly face. Diane listened carefully to the teacher and watched how the other children reacted. She had enough of standing out before in school due to her lack of decent clothing and being unclean. She just wanted to mix with the other children. The lack of schooling had an impact and Diane did struggle a little, despite listening well. She had been lucky, being put next to Lisa, who was bright and could see she was struggling with the sums. Lisa whispered the answers and Diane smiled gratefully.

Meanwhile, Jo wasn't faring so well. She struggled to see the blackboard and had experienced so little time in school that she lacked the discipline to stay in her seat and sometimes wandered around the classroom. Fortunately, Miss Tibbs was an experienced and kind teacher and had been advised that Jo had barely spent time in a classroom, so was tolerant of the little girl. The children were given an exercise book and asked to draw a picture. Jo looked confused, "What's this for the missus?"

Miss Tibbs replied, "It's Miss Tibbs, not missus."

Jo frowned, "Well, you better give her book back then, missus." Some of the other children started laughing and Jo glared at them, "What you lot laughing at?" Miss Tibbs managed to calm the class and little Jo, and explained to her about drawing a picture and showed her how to hold a pencil. There was a box of coloured pencils in a tub for each cluster of desks.

A little boy called Harry suggested Jo use another colour as she had been drawing her picture in a brown colour. Jo looked amazed at the way the colours looked on the paper and happily scribbled away.

Jeffrey, another boy, said, "Miss, she's just scribbling."

Jo stared at him, "Well, at least it's pretty colours."

Miss Tibbs smiled to herself, thinking, "We have a lively one here."

At playtime, the girls met in the playground. Diane had become friends with Lisa and brought her with her. Jo looked a little put out, "Who's she?" Diane introduced her friend Lisa who smiled at the frowning Jo.

Lisa suggested they play a game of mums and dads with Jo being the baby. Jo hadn't experienced much in the way of imaginative play, apart from when they used to dream up what lovely food they could eat.

"I ain't no baby," she complained.

Diane corrected her, "You mean you aren't a baby."

Jo nodded at Diane, "Yeh, that's just what I said."

The bell rang and Diane said to Jo she would see her at dinner time.

"What the heck's that?" Jo asked.

Diane gritted her teeth, Jo could be so embarrassing at times and hissed at Jo, "Dinner, food." Both girls went back to their classes.

At lunchtime, both girls sat at the same table with Lisa. The food was basic but the girls ate every bit. The constant lack of food in their formative years resulted in them eating virtually anything that was given to them.

Both girls initially struggled to get into the routine of going to school. It turned out that Lisa lived nearby so the girls would walk to school with her. Diane liked having a friend. When living in the Forest of Dean, she never had the chance to make friends. But Jo did get jealous sometimes. She was used to having Diane to herself a lot of the time. Although Lisa was kind to both girls, some of the other pupils made fun of their accent, saying they couldn't understand them.

Initially, Diane struggled a little with the work, but her teacher would spend some extra time helping her and over the months, she started to catch up with her peers. Unfortunately, for Jo, the work didn't come that easy. They found out she needed glasses and was taken to an optician. The first day she wore them to school, she was teased by the other children. Also, she found it hard to concentrate and sit still. At times, this annoyed Miss Tibbs who declared she must have ants in her pants. Jo, having never heard that expression, was horrified and exclaimed, "There ain't no ants in my pants, missus!" The whole class erupted with laughter; you never knew what Jo would say next!

One day at playtime, Jo met Diane, who was without Lisa, as she was off school with flu. Jo pulled out a packet of crisps from her coat pocket. "Look what I got," she said proudly.

Diane looked worried, "Jo, where did you get that packet of crisps from?" Jo admitted she took them from David's satchel which had been on the hook in the cloakroom and open. Diane glared at her sister, "You stole them. That's really naughty. We will have to take them back."

Jo looked confused, "But why?" Diane explained they didn't belong to them and it was stealing, which could get you in prison.

Suddenly, David approached the girls, "Gimme back my crisps you took." Jo put her hand with the crisp packet behind her back.

Diane pleaded with Jo, "Just give him the crisps back, Jo." Reluctantly, Jo gave the packet of crisps back, which David took and pushed her before he left. Jo sulked, a little cross that Diane had stopped her from having the crisps.

Soon, school became a way of life for the girls and they settled into the routine. After the initial teasing and scrutiny from other children, the girls made friends. Both girls found their teachers to be kind and patient.

Even when Jo was outspoken and sometimes rude, the teacher would patiently explain the way things were done. Not used to a routine, both girls struggled to a certain extent. The teacher was surprised at how little the girls knew about sayings the names of items. Despite this, the girls did settle down and became used to school life.

By the time they reached half term, it was obvious the girls needed extra help. Jo now wore glasses and could see properly, which helped, as she could now see the writing on the blackboard.

Diane adapted to school life well, she enjoyed learning and thrived with the routine. Jo, however, didn't take to school very well at all and didn't really have much of an interest in learning. Jo had always been outspoken, even when it put her in danger with her birth parents at risk of a severe beating. Although she didn't take to reading like her older sister, she quickly learnt that the punishment for 'cheekiness' was nowhere near as severe. Without Diane in the class to stop her, Jo would be rude to the teacher and revelled in the giggles and shock her classmates displayed.

In the playground, the others would ask, "How could you? I wouldn't dare." Unfortunately, it got to the stage where Jo would answer back just to get a reaction from her teacher and the other children. So much so that a letter was sent to Aunt Bet and Uncle Bertie.

When the social worker, Amanda, next came to visit them, Bet showed her the letter and was upset. Sometimes on a school day, Amanda would pop in whilst the girls were at school to check if Bet and Bertie were alright and ensured they were adequately supported. Amanda offered to talk to Jo. Part of Amanda's job was to talk to each girl alone, so if they were worried about anything, they could tell her. The girls came home and were happy to see Amanda and rushed over to hug her. "Now, I need to talk to you girls, you first this time, Jo."

Jo made a face at Diane, "Ha! Me first…nah."

Diane pushed her, "Go on, you." When they were alone Amanda raised the issue of her answering back. Initially, Jo denied it hotly. Amanda waited for her to calm down and gently, but firmly, explained that her answering back and generally not cooperating was unfair on herself, the other children and the teacher. She advised that Jo was letting herself down and that her aunt and uncle were sad because of this. Amanda continued, "Jo, you and Diane have done so well, you have settled into your new life and if you carry on as you are, you are letting yourself down." Jo blinked back some tears and nodded, for once, not able to retaliate. Amanda smiled at the little girl and patted her arm gently. "You will get there, you are a survivor, Jo. Just show us how good you can be."

Jo took on board what had been said. She didn't change completely and stay quiet in class and sometimes she had a flare-up and would answer back, but it was saved more for when she felt things were unjust and didn't use it as a tool to show off to the class. After a while, she began to make some friends. Jo never really took to the academic side of school life but had friends who found she was a good ally and if she felt there had been an injustice would speak out for her friends. As she grew older, Jo would develop a wicked sense of humour.

Jo's classmates would be amazed at what she would say, and as a result, would look up to her when she used inappropriate language. One day, the teacher was asking the children what they had for tea the previous day. Unfortunately, Jo was soon in trouble again. Again, a note was sent home to Bet and Bertie. On Amanda's next visit, Bet raised their concerns. This time, Amanda spoke to the family together. She explained that Jo's teacher was concerned about Jo's language and carried on to say that Jo had told the teacher she had, "Shit with sugar on it for tea." She explained to the girls that it was not nice to say such words. Amanda asked why had she done this as she knew full well those were not nice words for a little girl to speak.

Jo couldn't bear the look of disappointed on Amanda's face and started to cry, "But that's what my mum used to say when I asked what was for tea." Diane put a protective arm around her sister saying, "She's right, Miss, that's what our mum would say."

Amanda put her arm around the distressed Jo, "Don't cry, Jo, it must be very hard for her, but those aren't nice words, are they? Aunt Bet and Uncle Bertie don't like to hear that sort of language. That might have been said in your previous home, but it's not a nice language for any little girl to use." As she glanced over Jo's head, she could see Bertie shaking where he was trying not to laugh and she had a job to not laugh as well.

One day, walking to school alone, Jo was surprised when a car drew up and parked next to her. A man wound down the window and said, "Hello." Jo was a little nervous, as she had a lot of experience of her dad's friends coming round intoxicated, being loud and aggressive. Jo walked off rapidly and was relieved to be home. She didn't know whether or not to tell Aunt Bet or Uncle Bertie, so once the girls were put to bed, she told Diane about it. Diane looked worried and said they should tell Aunt Bet, but Jo begged her not to. Jo felt she would be in trouble if she told. The following two days, on the way to school, the same car followed Jo. Then on the fourth day, the man offered her sweets if she would get into the car. Jo loved sweets but something about the way the man looked at her frightened her and she fainted. A couple of people ran up to the little girl and someone shouted, "Call the police." The man drove off rapidly. When the police arrived, they asked Jo about the man and what he looked like. Once she seemed to have recovered, the police took her to school. That night, Aunt Bet sat the girls down and warned them about the dangers of talking to strangers.

Due to the levels of neglect and lack of care, neither girls were warned about the stranger danger.

Due to the family being registered blind, Bet and Bertie were given help with caring for the girls. It was the half-term holidays and the social worker, Amanda, came to take the girls out. By now, the girls knew Amanda and had become fond of her. In the summer, Amanda had taken them to parks and Weston-Super-Mare. So, the girls were excited about where she would take them. As Amanda walked through the door, both girls rushed to greet her. Amanda grinned at their excited faces. They had changed a lot since she was allocated as their social worker. The girls looked healthier, had colour in their cheeks and some of the 'haunted' look and wariness was going. Both girls had blossomed well and responded well to a caring, loving and nurturing environment. They still had a lot to learn but both girls were adjusting well and blossoming under the love and care given by their aunt and uncle. "Guess where we are going today, girls?"

Amanda smiled at the girls who both shouted, "Where, where?" they cried. Amanda told them they were going to the pictures (now usually known as the cinema).

"What pictures? I don't want to look at pictures," grumbled Jo. Amanda laughed and explained to the girls what going to the pictures meant. So, the girls went to Henleaze Cinema and watched 101 Dalmations. Not having a television at home meant this was a real treat. Both enjoyed the film immensely and couldn't stop talking about it on the walk home. Diane felt happy as she had heard Lisa talk about going to the pictures, now she could tell her she had been as well. Diane felt that at last they were enjoying the treats and outings that other children took for granted.

Later that night, the girls discussed their trip to the cinema excitedly. Diane said, "Remember we used to imagine that Aunt Bet and Uncle Bertie would rescue us and now it's happened."

As both girls adjusted to their new lives, there was still the fear that their parents would demand to have them back. Sometimes they would have nightmares and wake up screaming or sometimes one of them would wet the bed. Their aunt and uncle kindly and patiently dealt with the situation as best they could. Uncle Bertie had unending patience and would spend ages soothing a distressed child. Amanda had advised them that the girls might have reactions like this due to the way they were treated by their birth parents. Bet and Bertie still didn't realise the extent of what had happened, but gradually, as the years rolled on, more information would be disclosed as memories and flashbacks surfaced.

During the half-term, Aunt Bet had another outing planned for the girls. However, this was not going to seem as fun as the pictures. Amanda had advised Bet they needed to see a dentist as soon as they could make an appointment. So, the girls went to see the dentist. Diane went first and seemed impressed with the dentist chair. Despite never having gone to a dentist, the girls' teeth only needed a polish. However, Jo was worried about seeing her sister go through the examination. Once Diane got off the chair, the dentist asked Jo to come and sit in the chair. Jo shook her head. "Come on young lady, I don't bite," the dentist joked. Jo shook her head again.

Aunt Bet gently prodded her, "Get up and do as you are told."

Jo shook her head, "I can't." Aunt Bet continued to try and persuade her to get off her seat. Eventually, Jo stood up and the reason for her reluctance was clear. She had wet herself and was embarrassed about it. The dentist's assistant reassured them it was alright and she would clean it up. Aunt Bet was flustered and embarrassed and told Jo off when they walked home. For both girls, the telling off seemed a small punishment compared to what would have happened if they had been with their parents.

# Chapter Thirteen

The summer months and autumn rolled by quickly and soon it was the beginning of December. In the shops, there were Christmas cards and presents on display. Both girls were mesmerised at the gaily decorated shops on Gloucester Road. A few weeks later a huge, decorated Christmas tree was in the school hall for both children and at assembly the children would start to learn Christmas carols. On the last day of term, both girls enjoyed a Christmas party at their school. It was the first party they went to. For the occasion, Aunt Bet had bought them both a pretty party dress each. Diane's was pale blue and white and she had matching ribbons. Jo's dress was a similar style in red and white, again with matching ribbons.

Amanda had popped in to see the girls. Both looked pretty with their dresses and ribbons. She had agreed to take the girls to the school party. Amanda handed Bet a card and a present each for the girls to go under the tree. Aunt Bet encouraged the girls to say 'thank you.' Both girls ran to Amanda and hugged her, taking her by surprise. Amanda felt choked up. The girls were so different from the frightened, wary children she knew months ago. Seeing how the girls flourished now that they were taken care of properly was satisfying. The extra tuition the teacher gave was really helping the girls, especially Diane, who was quickly developing a love of reading. Although Jo didn't take to reading or writing, she was quick to pick up practical things and was a lively personality. Amanda felt if this was channelled in the right direction, things could go well for both girls. Amanda's job could be heart-breaking and really difficult at times, but seeing how these two small girls adapted and blossomed made her proud to be a social worker.

They had a way to go yet but they were adapting to a new lifestyle quickly. Amanda reminded them that she was taking them to see Father Christmas, she was a little surprised how little they reacted. For the girls, Father Christmas was an unknown quantity. Amanda explained who he was and how he delivered presents to all the good little girls and boys. Jo frowned, "Well, he never came to us."

Amanda paused and tried to think of how to answer this but Diane quickly intervened, "'Course he didn't, silly, we were living in the woods, he could never have found us there!"

Amanda smiled at the girls, "Well, he certainly knows where you live now."

Later, both girls returned home tired from their party. Aunt Bet told them to take off their dresses, wash and put on their nighties which were hanging by the coal fire to warm up. The two giggly girls were put to bed and Bet and Bertie could hear them talking and giggling. "Those girls, I will go and tell them to be quiet," muttered Bet.

Bertie held out an arm to stop her, "Leave them be. They have had such a miserable time in the past, let them enjoy themselves."

Bet frowned at Bertie, "You're too soft with them."

Bertie smiled, "So are you, love. So are you."

During the Christmas holidays, Amanda took the girls into town to see Father Christmas. In the past, Father Christmas would have not featured in their lives and they wouldn't have known him. However, with the celebrations at school and talking to other children, both girls had more of an idea of who he was. They queued in Jones' department store in Broadmead, both enthralled at the decorations in the store leading to Father Christmas' place. Amanda smiled at the way their eyes lit up. It was times like this when she found her job rewarding, seeing children who were abused or neglected enjoy the same things most other children have.

When they eventually got to see Father Christmas, both girls were a little shy. Due to their previous experiences, they both had a little fear of men they didn't know and here was a larger-than-life character dressed in bright red. Jo clutched hold of Diane's hand. Father Christmas addressed the girls, "Ho ho ho! Who do we have here then?" Amanda encouraged the girls to walk up to him. The girls shyly gave their names. Amanda lifted both girls on a knee each and he asked them what they wanted for Christmas. Jo said she wanted a dolly and he asked if Diane wanted a dolly too. Diane shook her head, for some reason she didn't like dolls. Diane volunteered she would like some books.

Both girls were given a gift. Jo wanted to open hers immediately so Amanda said they could. They had a yo-yo each. "What the heck's that?" exclaimed Jo.

Diane prodded her sister and hissed, "Don't be so rude." Amanda showed the girls how to play with their yo-yos on the bus going home. She smiled, thinking how excited the girls were just having a simple toy and wondered if there would be an excitement overload when Christmas Day came.

It was Christmas Eve and, in the morning, relatives came to visit to help with preparations. Amanda had taken Bet and the girls food shopping and helped trim up the house. The girls loved the festive Christmas tree and enjoyed drinking their cocoa in front of the warm coal fire. They loved the sparkly Christmas tree with the festive coloured lights.

The scene was so different than their previous home in the caravan where it was dismal, cold and frightening. Most of the time, the girls felt and tried to stay invisible, especially when their dad had been drinking, you never knew what would happen. Here, it was so different and especially with the relatives there as well, there were jokes and laughter and although some were drinking, they seemed jolly and not sullen or unpredictable. One of the uncles picked Jo up and danced around the room, she screamed in delight and giggled. Aunt Bet tutted, "Don't get her over-excited. I'll never get her to sleep." The uncle duly popped Jo back on the floor. Diane was tired and yawned loudly. Aunt Bet took her cue and decided it was bedtime. After kissing the girls goodnight and tucking them into bed, she closed the door.

"What do you go and yawn for? I was having fun," grumbled Jo. Diane turned her back on her sister and told her to go to sleep or Father Christmas wouldn't come.

The next morning, Jo shook her sister awake, "Wake up, let's go downstairs and see if he's been."

Diane rubbed her eyes and slowly got up. Suddenly, a worrying thought crossed her mind, what if it wasn't true? What if they were being teased as they did at home? She remembered coming home from school when they lived in the woods. She had become excited, really believing Father Christmas would bring them something and, as usual, was disappointed. When her older brother found out, he just laughed and told their mother who had looked scornfully at the disappointed little girl, saying, "Why would he bring you anything?"

Jo grabbed Diane's arm, pulling her out of her reverie. Diane fervently hoped that they wouldn't be disappointed this time, as Jo would be so upset.

The girls crept downstairs quietly and walked into the living room and to their amazement, on each armchair was a doll surrounded by piles of brightly, festive parcels. Both girls were amazed, "Are these really for us, Diane?"

Diane went over to a sofa with the doll wearing a red dress, the nearby parcels had Jo's name on them. "These are yours, Jo, they have your name on them." The other armchair with the blue dress was Diane's presents. For a few moments, both girls stared at the presents in awe. Although they had received presents from their aunt and uncle in the past, they had never had this much.

Then, they heard a noise and saw their aunt and uncle in the doorway. "Merry Christmas, girls. Have you opened your presents yet?" Uncle Bertie asked. Bet told him they hadn't touched them yet and encouraged the girls to open the parcels.

As soon as she knew it was alright, Jo hastily started opening the presents, leaving a pile of ripped wrapping paper on the floor.

Diane took her time opening the wrapping carefully, almost reverently. She seemed to relish opening the paper slowly, wondering what was inside. The presents for the girls were similar, they had their dolls, books, writing pads and coloured pencils. Some of the presents contained clothes. Both girls had a new outfit to wear for Christmas day with matching ribbons, new underwear and nightdresses. Diane had a light green check dress with white colour and Jo had the same in pink. Jo loved her dress and wanted to wear it straight away, but was told by Aunt Bet she needed to wash first. Although the girls had been with their aunt and uncle a while, the regular washing and bathing was something they were still getting used to.

Aunt Bet looked at the girls, who both looked lovely in their clothes, with their hair tied in bunches and their smiling faces. Bet had asked Amanda the social worker about clothes and she had gone out to buy them for her. As she looked at them, Bet realised how they had changed. When they came to her, their clothes were virtually ragged and the girls had ingrained dirt and looked terribly neglected. Almost as if they were orphans from the Victorian era. But looking at them now, they looked well and healthy. Both had put on weight and looked happy. Feeling a little emotional, Bet thought how angelic the girls looked, and dabbed her eyes with a hanky only to be brought back to earth by Jo's voice heard shouting at Diane, "Bugger off, that's mine," as she snatched a puzzle from Diane's hand.

"I was only looking, no need to shout or snatch."

Aunt Bet told Jo off for snatching and the bad language. *So much for looking like angels,* thought Aunt Bet as she encouraged the girls to pick up the empty wrappings which were strewn over the floor.

Later, the relatives arrived and the girls experienced their first proper Christmas. The table was full of people sat around and the girls had never seen such a large amount of food. Jo looked at the table with rounded eyes. After they ate, the girls received a few more presents.

Bet felt pride at how they remembered their manners and said, "Thank you."

Both girls loved their presents and could not believe how many they had.

After the meal, some of the adults had some alcohol, the men indulged in a whiskey or brandy and the women drank sherry. At first, the girls felt a little wary of this, anticipating that the adults would become nasty with the alcohol inside them. But to their surprise, the adults didn't become surly or brooding and still seemed happy and cheerful and encouraging the girls to show them their presents.

After a long day of present unwrapping, eating, and playing board games, which a relative helped them learn, by bedtime, both girls were tired. After their bath, they changed into their new nightdresses and sat by the fire drinking their cocoa before going to bed. Jo wouldn't let go of her doll and when they went to bed, she noticed that Diane had barely looked at her doll. "Why don't you play with your dolly?" Diane shook her head. There was something about dolls she didn't like and she was too young to understand why. So, Diane's doll stayed in the bedroom corner and she rarely touched it. Sometimes, she would let Jo play with it to be a sister to her doll. Jo liked to pretend the dolls were twins, as there were twins in her class and that fascinated Jo. Whilst Jo enjoyed the make-believe with the dolls, Diane preferred a book or puzzle.

As they settled into bed, Jo asked, "Will this still be here when we wake up?" Jo had made a good point, as often presents had been taken from the girls before they had a chance to play with them. Diane sleepily said the presents would still be there in the morning and hoped she was right.

# Chapter Fourteen

The girls flourished in their aunt and uncle's care. Food was no longer scarce; they were clean and healthy. Their social worker continued to be in their lives, helping them and their aunt and uncle. They soon became used to school life and made friends with other children at their school. But the sisters remained close to one another and if one of them was upset or hurt, they would turn to their sister rather than anyone else.

Occasionally, their oldest brother, Frank, would come and stay for a few days. But then he would go back home. Frank never volunteered much information about home life and the girls didn't ask. Diane sometimes wondered why they didn't, it was as if talking about it they would end up back with them and neither girl wanted that. They were accustomed to being clean, well dressed and fed properly. Both girls started taking an interest in their appearance and would experiment doing different hairstyles, which their social worker had shown them and played 'hairdressers' trying different bobbles and ribbons. Sometimes, the girls had mixed feeling about seeing their brother. They wanted to see him, but it would then bring back unpleasant memories. Quite often, one of the girls would have a nightmare following a visit from him.

The girls were aged seven and eight years by now. It was a Friday and they had gone to bed and were just drifting off to sleep when a heavy knock was heard on the door. Bertie answered the door and they heard their parents' voices. Both girls sat bolt upright in bed and Jo climbed out of her bed and got into Diane's bed, they held each other shaking with fear. The adult voices became louder with their father demanding to see them, backed up by their mother shouting.

"What if they take us? I don't want to go back with them." Diane shushed her sister up, as she wanted to hear what was being said. Diane was worried that her aggressive parents would barge past their uncle and would snatch them. Bertie was always the calmer, gentle guardian. Bertie then raised his voice, telling the parents he would not allow them in to see the girls and that if they had a problem with that then they would need to contact the children's department (Social Services). He shut the door and told Bet what had happened, although she could hear from the raised voices.

Bet got out of her chair to go upstairs and see how the girls were. When she went into the bedroom there was no sign of the girls on their bed, "Girls, girls where are you? It's alright they have gone now." After a few moments, both girls emerged from their hiding place under Diane's bed, both faces streaked with tears.

Bet sat on the bed and encouraged them to sit either side of her, so she could reassure them all was alright with a cuddle. As she held the two girls, Uncle Bertie came in, "How are my two girls? It's alright, they've gone."

Diane looked up and said, "We were scared they would take us back to the forest. We don't want to go; we want to stay with you and Aunt Bet."

Bet addressed the girls, "You can both stay with us forever. We won't ever let you go as long as you want to stay with us."

Jo looked up, "Can we call you Mummy and Daddy?" Bet looked surprised and didn't know what to say, so paused.

Bertie interrupted the awkward silence, "Yes, of course, you can girls. You are our girls now." Bet looked sharply at Bertie and was a little worried what the children's welfare office would say. She had grown to love these two girls and didn't want anything to stop them from caring for them. They couldn't go back to their parents. Bet then turned her attention back to the girls and tucked them in bed.

As she kissed them goodnight, they both said, "Goodnight, Mummy." Bet left the bedroom with tears in her eyes. After that, the girls referred to their aunt and uncle as Mum and Dad.

As they talked, Bet told Bertie off for agreeing to say they could be called 'Mum and Dad', "What if the social worker gets annoyed and takes them away? You know they have some funny ideas, these social workers."

Bertie tried to reassure her that it would be fine, "After all, we have been more like parents to them than those two good-for-nothing parents. At least with us, they have learnt things and know what a clock is. They were only surviving in that forest and not living." Bet agreed, looking back on those first few months, trying to encourage the girls to bathe and showing them the simplest of things and establishing a routine.

Neither girl could read when they came to them. Fortunately, due to both girls having good, understanding teachers, they were beginning to catch up. Diane had developed a love of books and was delighted when she was introduced to a library and enjoyed being taken there by Amanda.

Since the girls moved in with their aunt and uncle, the truth about the neglect and abuse had come out. When the girls learnt they could trust them, stories of what happened when they lived with their birth parents came out. Although Bet was aware things were difficult, she had no idea the extent of it. Bet was shocked and sickened by the tales and chided herself for not noticing the extent of the abuse. She often marvelled that the girls were still alive, such was the abuse they suffered. However, Francis and Rita were very sly and had managed to keep up a façade of family life, with the only issue being a lack of money. Both were practised at conning both relatives and professionals.

Bet was shocked that the presents and clothes she used to give them were sold for alcohol and that the parents had put their own needs before their children. Things that most children took for granted, Diane and Jo had never seen. Sometimes, the girls would react in an unusual way, such as when they misbehaved and she had to tell them off, Jo would cover her head with her arms. Bet was shocked when Diane explained that one of their mother's punishments was to drag them by the hair and lock them in a cupboard. In the first few months, both girls hoarded some of the food, worried where their next meal would come from. Fortunately, Amanda explained this was common for children suffering neglect and gave them advice on how to deal with it and help reassure the girls that they would not go hungry. After months of reassurance from Bet and Amanda, the girls realised that this wasn't like their previous experiences and that they would be fed regularly.

Bet recalled their aversion to having their first bath, especially Jo, who had really made a fuss about it and now it was difficult getting her out of the bath. As the girls settled into their lives with Bet and Bertie, they changed, not only physically but emotionally. At first, they were so frightened and wary that it was as if they existed as one person and not two, but gradually, as they settled, and became more comfortable, it was surprising how different they were. Diane would consider her actions before reacting to anything and weigh up the pros and cons, whereas impulsive Jo would rush in and react. The girls developed different interests; Diane liked reading and doing puzzles, whereas Jo loved her dolls. They had similar interests, such as going to the pictures and considered this a real treat.

Their brothers would come and stay for a few days in the summer holidays. Although this maintained ties with their siblings, it sometimes caused some problems and sometimes the girls would suffer from flashbacks and a fear they would be taken back to their parents.

When the girls were aged nine and ten, Amanda came to take them to the council offices, called the Council House at the time. She led the girls into an office and then explained to them that their birth parents were in the next office and had come to see them. Both girls looked at each other in shock. They hadn't seen their parents since Benny took them away. Diane felt a turmoil, she was at an age where she was becoming curious about their lives and wanted answers as to why they were treated so harshly and why their parents didn't care for them. Why had they neglected and abused them, when other parents loved their children and would do anything for them. With all these conflicting thoughts in her head, she looked at Jo, who looked angry, glaring at the social worker with her arms folded.

Amanda prompted the girls, "So, girls, do you want to see your parents? I will stay with you. You will be perfectly safe with me there." Diane felt confused and didn't know what to say, as she felt a mixture of curiosity and fear. Before she could respond, Jo stood up, grabbed Diane's hand and started walking towards the door. Amanda looked surprised, "Jo, what are you doing are you going to see them?"

Jo stopped and frowned at Amanda, "No, they are dead to us. Come on, Diane, let's go home." So, with that, both girls and the social worker left the offices without seeing the birth parents. From that day onwards, the girls referred to Aunt Bet and Uncle Bertie as Mum and Dad.

Over the years, the birth parents occasionally turned up wanting to see the girls and were refused access. When Diane was 15, her parents visited and asked to have them back, as Diane was old enough to go out and work. She flatly refused to go with them, despite their feeble excuses of what a good life she could have with them. Her father tried to persuade her that things had changed and that they had missed the girls and wanted them back. Francis could put on the charm when he thought it was to his advantage and tried this with the girls. Diane glared at him, saying, "We know what kind of life we had with you two. Thanks to the way we were treated, we are likely to never forget. So, no we won't go with you. Our home is here, with our mum and dad."

# Epilogue

Both girls spent the rest of their childhood with their aunt and uncle, who they referred to as Mum and Dad. Bet and Bertie showed the girls love, kindness, and appropriate boundaries, which was such stark difference to their previous home life and the brutality that prevailed. The girls were taught how to live properly and not just exist and for that, they were eternally grateful to their aunt and uncle. It was only after moving in with their uncle and aunt that their education began properly and they were able to live like ordinary people.

For Bet and Bertie, it was a chance to love and care for children, as they had no children of their own. As the girls grew older and felt safe to talk about their lives with their birth parents, Bet realised the misgivings she had when visiting had been correct. She tried not to think about what might have happened if the girls had not come into their care. Bet spent many nights feeling upset as information about the girls' lives came out.

Both girls left school and obtained jobs. In time, they both got married. Diane and her husband had a son and continued living with Bet and Bertie. Jo married and had a daughter and lived close by. Bet and Bertie then enjoyed having their grandchildren around. For both girls, 'family' became a word to be celebrated rather than feared.

Despite their differences in personality, both Diane and Jo lived close to one another and are still close as sisters now. Both are now grandparents and enjoy their time with their children and grandchildren. They kept in touch with their social worker, Amanda, who attended both of their weddings and was regarded as a close family friend.

Their oldest brother, Frank, remained with his parents until they died.

Both sisters kept in touch with their brother, John, and over recent years, they re-established contact with their other brother, Jack.

Both Jo and Diane often wondered what life would have been like if they had remained with their birth parents and how they would have survived if they had remained in their care. However, the vivid memory of their early life still haunts them and there are a lot of unanswered questions as to why their early years were so neglectful and brutal. However different they are, both are strong and are survivors.

Being rescued by their aunt and uncle showed them how a proper family lived; with love, care and patience, the little girls blossomed into hard-working, caring and loving parents.

**The End**

CPSIA information can be obtained
at www.ICGtesting.com
Printed in the USA
LVHW090441110721
692308LV00001BB/1

9 781528 954419